The Persona Book

The Persona Book

Curriculum-Based Enrichment
for Educators

Katherine Grimes Lallier
Library Media Specialist,
Robert W. Carbonaro Elementary School, Valley Stream, NY

and

Nancy Robinson Marino
Assistant Professor,
C. W. Post Campus, Long Island University, Brookville, NY

1997
Teacher Ideas Press
A Division of
Libraries Unlimited, Inc.
Englewood, Colorado

For John, James, and Erin
KGL

For Sal
NRM

Copyright © 1997 Katherine Grimes Lallier and Nancy Robinson Marino
All Rights Reserved

No part of this publication may be reproduced, stored in a retrieval system, or transmitted, in any form or by any means, electronic, mechanical, photocopying, recording, or otherwise, without the prior written permission of the publisher. An exception is made for individual librarians and educators, who may make copies of activity sheets for classroom use in a single school. Other portions of the book (up to 15 pages) may be copied for in-service programs or other educational programs in a single school or library. Standard citation information should appear on each page.

TEACHER IDEAS PRESS
A Division of
Libraries Unlimited, Inc.
P.O. Box 6633
Englewood, CO 80155-6633
1-800-237-6124
www.lu.com/tip

Production Editor: Kay Mariea
Copy Editor: Thea De Hart
Proofreader: Eileen Bartlett
Typesetter: Kay Minnis

Library of Congress Cataloging-in-Publication Data

Lallier, Katherine Grimes, 1960-
  The persona book : curriculum-based enrichment for educators / Katherine Grimes Lallier and Nancy Robinson Marino.
    x, 193p. 22x28 cm.
    Includes bibliographical references.
    ISBN 1-56308-443-0
    1. History--Study and teaching (Elementary)--United States--Curricula. 2. Role playing. 3. Education, Elementary--Activity programs--United States. 4. United States--History--Study and teaching (Elementary)--Curricula. 5. Persona (Literature)
I. Marino, Nancy Robinson, 1960-   .   II. Title.
LB1582.U6L35   1997
372.89--DC21   96-37655
                                                               CIP

Contents

ACKNOWLEDGMENTS vii

INTRODUCTION ix

Part One

A General Guide to Persona-Based Curriculum Enrichment 1

   What Is Persona-Based Enrichment? 2
   Role Playing 3
   What Is a Persona? 4
   Types of Personas 4
   The Literature Base 4
   Cooperation Between Teacher and Librarian 5
   The Organization of Persona-Based Enrichment Projects 6
   Persona Work Sheet 9
   Dramas 9
   Activities and Games 10
   Conclusion 10
   References 10

Part Two

1—CAMELOT ALIVE: Introducing the Middle Ages Through the Legends of King Arthur 11

   Camelot Alive 12
   The Personas of King Arthur's Court 12
   Step One: Prepersona Activities 16
   Step Two: Decision Making 17
   Step Three: Discovery Period 20
   Culminating Activities 21
   Bibliography 41

v

2—MOUNT OLYMPUS REVISITED: Exploring Ancient Greece Through Olympian Myths ... 43

Mount Olympus Revisited ... 44
The Personas of Mount Olympus ... 44
Step One: Prepersona Activities ... 50
Step Two: Decision Making ... 51
Step Three: Discovery Period ... 54
Culminating Activities ... 55
Bibliography ... 79

3—VALLEY OF THE KINGS: Discovering Ancient Egypt Through Its Mythology ... 81

Valley of the Kings ... 82
The Personas of Ancient Egypt ... 82
Step One: Prepersona Activities ... 86
Step Two: Decision Making ... 87
Step Three: Discovery Period ... 88
Culminating Activities ... 93
Bibliography ... 114

4—VOICES OF THE CIVIL WAR: Understanding the Civil War Through a Variety of Sources, Including Historical Fiction and Biography ... 117

Voices of the Civil War ... 118
Voices of the Civil War Persona List ... 118
Step One: Prepersona Activities ... 122
Step Two: Decision Making ... 123
Step Three: Discovery Period ... 126
Culminating Activities ... 129
Bibliography ... 154

5—AMERICAN HEROES FOR OUR TIMES: Defining America as a Nation Through the Attributes of Outstanding Americans ... 157

American Heroes for Our Times ... 158
Biography Personas ... 158
Step One: Prepersona Activities ... 161
Step Two: Decision Making ... 162
Step Three: Discovery Period ... 162
Culminating Activities ... 165
Bibliography ... 190

ABOUT THE AUTHORS ... 193

ACKNOWLEDGMENTS

A project, like a garden, starts with a seed. With dedication and hard work, it grows to have a life of its own. Each curriculum unit was like that seed, starting with an idea, and then growing and changing as each educator placed her unique mark on the units. These projects were truly a collaborative effort—as all good education should be. We would like to thank the dedicated staff at the Robert W. Carbonaro Elementary School in Valley Stream, New York—especially those who helped create the projects in this book: Laurie Arnone, Joan Centor, Faye Egre, Patty Horowitz, Marcia Jones, Dianne McKeon, Linda Melluso, Carrie Richman, Marie Shea, Anne Sheppard, Andrea Sommella, and Mady Tiktin.

To the Valley Stream Teacher Center: Through their minigrant program, three of the five units were given financial backing to further develop the library collection and make these projects possible.

To Suzanne Feldberg: For enhancing the book with her wonderful artwork.

To Dorothy Pantason: For capturing these projects on film.

To Marie Shea: For her clever Pharaoh rap.

To Jane Quaglin: For her insight and suggestions.

To Richard Lord: For his Civil War expertise.

To Lea Michos: For providing us with an authentic Greek folk dance.

To Talents Unlimited: For the use of their decision-making technique.

There are two educators who deserve special thanks and without whom these units never would have been realized.

To Laurie Celona Arnone: A colleague and close friend. She exemplifies an educator who looks for exciting ways to present the curriculum to students. She is also an innovative teacher, a risk taker, and a consummate professional; she helped develop these projects before anyone knew if they would really work.

To Dorothy Pantason: A friend and mentor for her encouragement and guidance. Her enthusiasm and dedication is inspirational. As the enrichment resource teacher, she motivates students and teachers to strive for a higher level. Each of these units was given the indispensable "Dorothy" stamp of excellence.

INTRODUCTION

Experience is the best teacher. If you want to learn about sea life, all the books in the world cannot compare with the sights, touch, and sound of the seashore, the feeling of coming face-to-face with a shark in an aquarium, or the excitement of exploring an underwater coral reef. As educators, we constantly strive to bring experiences into our classrooms and school libraries. But how can you get children to experience a 2,000-year-old event or culture, one that has long since become only a page in a history book? How do you bring to life the Middle Ages, the Civil War, or ancient Greece? Museums provide artifacts and tangible evidence of a culture, but they do not give children a true feeling for life in that period, and in many cases, the enthusiasm for the time period only lasts as long as the class trip. How then do you keep children involved and encourage them to become active learners and lovers of history?

This book presents a program, "persona-based enrichment," that is designed to enhance students' knowledge of historical curriculum-content areas by combining literature-based enrichment and role playing. The program is effective in bringing the past to life for students and in allowing them to become immersed in literature. It also promotes higher-level thinking, enhances self-esteem, and is fun. Children become active participants instead of passive learners. What better way to introduce children to the Middle Ages than through the legends of King Arthur or to learn about the secrets of ancient Egypt than through the myths of that period? But providing a literature base to curriculum-content areas is only the first step of the enrichment program. Children are provided with an incentive to learn even more. They choose a character, or "persona"—either historical or mythological—from the literature and create colorful projects and participate in events as that persona. Having students imagine themselves as actual literary figures is a powerful way to immerse them in a period and gives purpose to their research and learning experiences.

This book is divided into two parts, one of which explains persona-based enrichment. It presents a guideline for all persona projects and provides information and hints for using this as a curriculum-enrichment tool. The book's second and larger part consists of enrichment units. They are presented for various curriculum-content areas and are targeted at grades four through seven. Each unit lets students explore a particular aspect of history. For example, students springboard off Arthurian legends to create medieval personas and perform in a theater-in-the-round. In another unit they absorb Greek culture and mythology through participation in the first Olympics, or their biography project could be a talk show, with host Matthew Henson and guests Abraham Lincoln, Amelia Earhart, and Diego Rivera. These are just some of the ways to use persona-based projects to enrich students' learning experiences.

Each enrichment unit contains a literature base, performance recommendations, and a list of personas. Because it is the source for the personas, the literature is an important element. The school media specialist, therefore, plays a vital role in bringing this enrichment experience to the students. Bibliographies are provided with each chapter as a further aid. Certain books are highlighted within each chapter with suggestions on how to incorporate them into the unit.

The projects and performances for each enrichment unit range from creating persona books to writing and directing a commercial. All projects give purpose to the research by providing a meaningful and fun incentive. A list of personas is also provided for each unit and includes a thumbnail sketch of every character. If the character is not especially well known, the literary work in which the character can be found is noted. When it is appropriate we have provided suggestions for incorporating computers into the projects.

These projects have been student tested using large and small groups. All types of learners—from the learning disabled to the gifted—have participated. All types of personalities—from the most reticent to the most outgoing—have enjoyed this form of enrichment. The results have been enormously successful. We hope you and your students try a persona-based enrichment project, and we wish you great success.

Part One

A General Guide to Persona-Based Curriculum Enrichment

What Is Persona-Based Enrichment?

Curriculum enrichment includes any projects, experiences, or activities that extend or enhance the curriculum. Persona-based projects enable students to become active learners and can enrich learning by providing a truly purposeful educational experience.

Persona-based enrichment has two goals: to immerse students in literature, allowing them to explore literature across the curriculum-content area; and, through active learning, to familiarize students with a particular curriculum-content area. Persona-based enrichment begins when a student chooses a persona. But before this can occur, the student is exposed to the literature of the period by the teacher reading aloud to the students several books about the specific subject or period. All the students then have a common frame of reference, are introduced to the personas, and have a taste for the period they will be researching. Each student then chooses a persona and begins research knowing that he or she will be participating in a project or an event as that persona. So if a child decides while studying biographies that he would like to take on the persona of Abraham Lincoln, then as part of one of the culminating projects for the unit he would role-play as the president and, along with other students, would simulate a television talk show. To participate fully in the event, the student must know who Abraham Lincoln was, what part he played in the Civil War, and even, if possible, what he liked for breakfast. The student must synthesize and evaluate this new knowledge in preparation for the performance so that he might field any question—after all, one of the questions that any talk-show host would ask Lincoln is what he thinks of our current president.

Persona-based enrichment:

1. Promotes higher-level thinking. According to Bloom's Taxonomy of Cognitive Domain, the higher levels of thinking are analysis, synthesis, and evaluation. By participating in culminating projects as a persona, students function on these higher levels. They must take their knowledge of their persona's culture and personality and decide how that persona would act in various situations.

2. Immerses students in a particular culture or civilization by dramatizing an event from that time. Students engage in learning situations that promote creativity and generate enthusiasm for the curriculum-content area and the learning process.

3. Introduces students to quality literature. Exposure to the literature involves everything from reading aloud to students to watching video adaptations.

4. Integrates literature into the curriculum. Students have an added incentive to explore the literature being presented because it is where the personas originate.

5. Encourages cooperation. Personas must exist within an environment and interact with others within that environment. Students play off one another's personas, and because children are acting as someone other than themselves, even the most reserved child might be more inclined to interact with others.

6. Enlists students to become effective users of information. To research their personas, students must engage in a variety of information-seeking processes, including learning how to use print sources, indexes, books, and CD-ROMs. Through exploring personas, students learn about the research process.

7. Invites individuality. Each student has his or her own persona and is encouraged to express it in any way. Final projects can include many mediums: drawing, music, video, writing, performing, painting, sculpting—the range of expression is limited only by the student's imagination.

Researching and developing a persona allows students to have enrichment at their own pace. Each student may develop the persona through his or her own special talent. All types of learners, from the gifted to the severely learning disabled, benefit from the enrichment process. In one persona-based enrichment project, one child, a gifted actor, mesmerized the class with his theatrical portrayal of King Arthur. Another child, a learning-disabled student, was able to portray her persona through costume and a mural. Her difficulties in verbal expression did not hamper her ability to express herself artistically. One boy who was emotionally challenged was so proud of his page on the Big Book of Personas that he asked to take it home—the first time that year he asked to take any of his work home. An obvious by-product of the students' enthusiasm is increased self-esteem.

Children are presented with a variety of ways to express themselves. Drawing, painting, acting, writing, researching, planning, and organizing are only some of the skills needed to create a persona project. The diversity of expression accommodates various learning styles; therefore, the students are more likely to meet with success.

They benefit as well from the opportunity to work on the projects either in groups or as a class. Together their personas create a moment from history, yet individually, in the present, each student has the opportunity to create something unique. No other student has the same persona, and so every contribution to the group project is original.

Role Playing

Having each student select a persona from history or literature encourages active participation in the project. Role playing is an important part of persona-based enrichment. Mark Chesler and Robert Fox state that role playing "calls for a student's stepping outside the accustomed role that he plays in life, relinquishing his usual patterns of behavior for the role and patterns of another person. This other role may be real or entirely fictitious" (Chesler and Fox 1966, 3). Fannie and George Shaftel concur, adding that "role playing permits one to put oneself in the other's shoes, to decenter, step out of one's own view, momentarily, and see things from another person's viewpoint. . . . Role playing is an empathy process. By placing oneself in the role of another, we are often enabled to feel what it is like to be in the other's situation" (Shaftel and Shaftel 1982, 5). So by the student's playing a role, a historical, mythical, or fictitious character becomes real. The persona's environment becomes the student's environment; his or her problems become the student's problems. This gives the student an authentic reason to learn about a particular curriculum-content area.

In persona-based enrichment, role playing occurs from the moment the student chooses a persona and begins to learn about the particular culture through the eyes of someone of that culture. Culminating projects extend role playing and provide the student with an individualized form of expression.

What Is a Persona?

Students need to understand the difference between a persona and a character in a play. The character in a play must read written lines and memorize the script. The character's thoughts and feelings are determined by the playwright and the director. Having children create a persona is different and requires children to function at a much higher level of thinking. Students must research their chosen personas by reading stories and studying the period in which the persona lived. Rather than merely acting out a part in a play, students, based upon their reading, become legendary characters or famous people, exhibiting all the traits that appear in the literature or history. Bits of information must be gathered from a variety of sources and synthesized into a unique being. Although students are bound by the stories and historical period, they can still give much of themselves to their personas. Students must be comfortable enough with the characters that they need not follow a script. Instead, each student must understand how his or her persona would react in any situation. For example, what would King Tutankhamen think of Howard Carter, the archaeologist who found his tomb? The child must know stories of the period to project how the persona would behave.

Types of Personas

A persona is usually a specific character or figure in history. It can be a medieval knight or a Greek god. It can be a real figure or an imaginary one. Sometimes a child may not choose to be any specific character but a general persona. For example, some students may decide they want to be knights in the Middle Ages instead of specific characters. Such general choices present advantages and disadvantages. A general persona, such as a serf or knight, allows a child to explore the culture and create his or her own persona based on his or her knowledge of that culture. The student develops this persona, giving that persona a personality, a name, and a life story. Students are allowed to express themselves creatively yet are bound by a particular time in history.

On the other hand, picking a specific character allows the child to understand a distinct individual. By following the life or legends of a specific mythological figure, a student will come to understand the complexities and interrelationships of a particular collection of myths. By choosing a persona who is a specific historical figure, the student will come to understand that person's contribution to history as well as that figure's human frailties and attributes. This leads to an appreciation that history is made by people who are not simply names in a textbook.

The Literature Base

Students become immersed in the literature throughout the projects. Any genre of literature can be used as the basis for a persona-based project. The curriculum-content areas described in the following chapters offer a variety of literary genres from biographies to historical fiction to traditional tales. Traditional literature is used in several of the projects, including "Camelot Alive," "Mount Olympus Revisited," and "Valley of the Kings." According to Carol Lynch-Brown and Carl M. Tomlinson, traditional literature includes myths, folktales, and legends that have been passed down through time by oral tradition and are eventually written down (Lynch-Brown and Tomlinson 1993).

Introducing traditional literature to children is of value, reason Lynch-Brown and Tomlinson, because:

- Traditional stories are highly entertaining. . . . The action is immediate and the characters are easy to love and hate.

- Traditional literature is an excellent source of storytelling.

- Hearing traditional stories helps children to develop a strong sense of story, which in turn provides them with a good foundation for understanding other literary genres.

- Knowing the characters and situations of traditional literature is part of being culturally literate.

- Traditional literature provides an interesting way for children to be introduced to the diverse cultural groups of their country and other countries (Lynch-Brown and Tomlinson 1993, 88-89).

Traditional literature lends itself to persona-based enrichment because it is rich in colorful characters, and the literature itself provides insight into a particular culture or historical period. Introducing the legends of King Arthur when learning about the Middle Ages or ancient myths when learning about the history of ancient Egypt or Greece is how traditional literature can be used to springboard into curriculum-content areas.

Another type of literature used is the biography, which students learn about when studying "American Heroes for Our Times." Students examine characteristics that make a person a hero by reading biographies. Through the biography personas they choose, they not only learn about the America in which the people lived but also are able to study a variety of information sources such as magazines, databases, and television.

Historical fiction is incorporated into the "Voices of the Civil War" chapter. While students portray the personas of real people, they are exposed to fiction that helps them learn about how war affects individuals. Historical figures make excellent personas and provide a basis for exploring an aspect of history. Whichever type of literature is chosen, students benefit from being introduced to various forms of literature that are incorporated into their curriculum.

Cooperation Between Teacher and Librarian

These projects encourage cooperation between the teacher and librarian. Students learn about the content area from the teachers in their classrooms, and the librarian introduces the literature base. Once students decide on their personas, the library becomes a pivotal place for discovering about the personas and the curriculum-content area. Other special-area teachers can be brought into these persona-based projects. Music, art, and physical education can all be integrated into these projects. For example, in "Camelot Alive," the physical education teacher can choreograph a Maypole dance.

The Organization of Persona-Based Enrichment Projects

Step One: Prepersona Activities

Each persona-based enrichment unit starts with the teacher or librarian reading literature aloud to the students. This familiarizes them with the particular area of study and introduces some of the personas. For the more difficult or important stories it enables all students to have a common frame of reference. An interesting story, one rich in adventure, can inspire students to learn more about the places or time period of that tale. But the benefits of reading any literature aloud to students—of any age—cannot be ignored. In their book *For Reading Out Loud: A Guide to Sharing Books with Children*, Margaret Mary Kimmel and Elizabeth Segel state that "reading aloud to children from literature that is meaningful to them has come to be widely acknowledged among experts to be the most effective, as well as the simplest and least expensive, way to foster in children a lifelong love of books and reading" (Kimmel and Segel 1988, 3).

Before reading a story to students, inform them that they will need to pick a persona for the unit. Children are then motivated to decide which persona they would like to be for their projects, and they listen to the stories and literature for details about each character.

When deciding which books to read aloud, the teacher or librarian should consider the personas in the project. Students should be exposed to as many of their personas as possible, and special emphasis should be placed on the lesser-known personas. For example, most students are familiar with King Arthur and Sir Lancelot, but probably few have heard of Sir Gawain. Reading the tale of "Sir Gawain and the Green Knight" introduces students to a new persona and treats them to an exciting adventure.

To familiarize students with role playing, each chapter lists a prepersona activity designed to encourage students to start thinking in the first person. In each chapter, a story is read aloud. Then either as a class or individually, students are asked to respond to questions about what is motivating a character to act in a certain way. Each question begins with "What if you were. . .," attempts to bring students outside of their normal frame of reference, and starts students thinking about what it would be like to encounter the same experiences as the character.

Step Two: Decision Making

Allowing students to choose their own personas increases their self-esteem and gives them an incentive to learn more about the particular time in history. A colorful variety of personas are provided in the following chapters. A student should be encouraged to pick the one that suits him or her best rather than having the teacher or librarian make the choice, because such a decision empowers the student and allows the child to take responsibility for his or her learning process. Having students take responsibility for their learning is critical to the success of all persona projects.

Inevitably, however, two or more students will want to be the same persona. There are no hard-and-fast rules against students choosing the same persona, but it may foster competition between them and create an especially uncomfortable learning experience if the abilities of the students vary greatly. Also, it takes away from the unique contribution that each child will make to the project. The decision-making element to this lesson provides a way to handle a situation in which two or more students want the same thing.

Each child must provide a rationale for wanting to be a particular persona. The teacher, librarian, and especially the child discover the particular motivation. In some instances, one student may have a more compelling reason for wanting to be a persona. For example, one student may write that he wants to be Lancelot because he is "loyal and brave," while the other may explain that he wants to be Lancelot because "my best friend, John, is King Arthur." To avoid such conflicts, students should choose more than one persona. Some students may then take their second choice, but the teacher or librarian should speak to each child individually to ensure that each student is satisfied with his or her choice of a persona.

Although choosing a persona is one of the motivating factors in this project, merely allowing a child to pick a role does not help the child extend his or her decision-making capabilities. One effective way for students to learn to verbalize their choice is for them to use specified criteria for decision making and to be able to articulate reasons why they want to be a specific persona. In the decision-making section of this enrichment program, any lesson that teaches decision-making skills can be implemented. *Talents Unlimited*, based on Calvin Taylor's multiple-talents approach, is especially effective. The lessons in the book concentrate on the decision-making aspect of the Talents Unlimited model, which provides students with a structure for choosing a persona and promotes decision-making skills. The decision-making aspect of the Talents model is a five-step approach that helps students to become effective decision makers.

1. Have students think of many possible things (alternatives).

2. Ask them to think more carefully about each of these things (criteria).

3. Ask students to review all the questions and to think carefully about their alternatives (weighing).

4. Let them choose one (decision).

5. Have them give many varied reasons for their choices (reasons).

The multiple-talents approach nurtures students' abilities in five talent areas: productive thinking, planning, communicating, forecasting, and decision making. For more information about Talents Unlimited, call (334) 690-8060.

Before the decision-making lesson, the students need to be acquainted with the major literary or historical figures dealt with in the unit. While there should be ample literature to sustain the unit, at the time of the decision-making lesson, the children should have a background in some of the literature and the curriculum-content area. Following are some strategies based on the Talents Unlimited model for the decision-making lesson.

1. Explain to students they will be doing projects as a persona, and they will be deciding which persona they want to be. They will be making three selections, and it is important they give many varied reasons for their choice. These reasons will be especially important if two or more students want to be the same persona.

2. Place a chart with the criteria for decision making in a visible place. Encourage students to invent additional criteria for decision making. Some general questions that may be used are:

    Do I like the persona of the character?

    Do I want to have a big part in a performance?

Will I do extra research concerning this character?

Will I be able to design and make the costume?

Can I give many reasons for my decision?

In the curriculum-content chapters, other examples of decision-making models are given.

3. If a performance is part of the culminating project, explain to students that these characters require more work and research. Some children will want a large part in the performance; others will look for roles that suit their individual styles.

4. Review the characters on the persona sheets. Emphasize the lesser-known literary characters or historical figures. Feel free to retell some stories.

5. Not all students will want to be a specific persona. For example, in the "Valley of the Kings" unit, a student may not care which character he or she is as long as he or she is an archaeologist. If there are not enough famous archaeologists to go around, the student may be satisfied to create a character who is one. The student will still have to research pyramids, mummies, and the culture of ancient Egypt to successfully create his persona.

6. Encourage students to make their own decisions. The choice should be the individual student's and not based on peer pressure.

7. Before allowing students to select their personas, meet with each student individually. It is important that every child is satisfied with his or her persona, especially if the student was not able to have his or her first choice.

Step Three: Discovery Period

Once each child has a persona, it is time for the student to use it to explore the particular time period. Students research and try to gather as much information as possible about their particular persona. Besides collecting anecdotes and stories about their own persona, they must delve into all aspects of a particular culture or environment. For example, if their persona lived in a castle in the Middle Ages, they must become experts about castles. In this way they are not only researching their own character but gathering, assimilating, and learning about the historical period. This is the primary purpose of their research: to learn about the historical period or curriculum-content area. The more students learn about the curriculum-content area, the more knowledge they have acquired about their persona.

Library time turns into discovery time. Students learn important research skills as they sift through books, databases, encyclopedias, fiction, and nonfiction for information about their personas. Each lesson they learn in the classroom contributes to their knowledge base as well. Students synthesize and evaluate all the knowledge presented to them, and slowly their personas start to emerge.

During this time, students plan their culminating projects, which are often centered around a general theme. For example, when studying ancient Greece, the culminating projects can center around the Olympics. Students can decide how they will express their own individual personas as well as participate in planning group activities.

Step Four: Culminating Projects

Each persona-based enrichment ends with one or several culminating projects. These projects give meaning to the research each student has done. Each chapter has examples of culminating projects. One or all can be used for each content area, or they can be used as a springboard for other ideas or projects. The only essential ingredient is that the culminating project incorporates the personas.

Listed below are culminating projects that can be done for any of the persona-based enrichment units. The culminating projects consist of dramas, activities and games, displays, and spectacles.

Persona Work Sheet

Each child is given a page to express his or her persona and is furnished with questions about the persona. These questions act as a skeleton for the students to build on in whichever way they choose. Variations on this work sheet as well as subject-specific questions are provided in the unit chapters. Students use the work sheet—the basis for many projects—as a guide to write about their persona. For example, in the "Mount Olympus Revisited" chapter, the work sheets along with the illustrations are placed together to make Athene's Quilt. In "Camelot Alive," the work sheets provide the basis for creating King Arthur's Big Book of Personas.

The most important characteristic of this exercise is that children can begin thinking about their persona in the first person. In drawing a picture of their persona, students need to think about how each persona dresses. If a performance or special dress-up day is to follow, these drawings help students think about their costumes. The Big Book of Personas is a great way for students to show off their knowledge and the research involved in exploring a specific theme or time period. It also allows students who may be shy to express themselves artistically.

Dramas

Most children enjoy performing, and it is a good way for students to role-play their personas. Ideally, it would be wonderful if all students wrote their own persona scripts. Some children are eager to do so and should be given the chance. Others may need encouragement. One aspect of the enrichment project is to give all students, regardless of their learning styles and abilities, the opportunity to feel good about participating in the project.

Students can perform from the prewritten scripts in the following chapters, or they can make up their own stories. Even with scripts, the child must decide how the character will react. The script can be used as a springboard. It provides a skeleton of boundaries for the children, but they should be encouraged to go beyond it. If a class is giving a performance using the scripts, avoid giving too much stage direction. Of course, some children may have to be told to speak louder, but it is important to let the child decide how the character will say the lines and react to those being said to him. Students bring their own experiences and use them to determine how their personas will react in a given situation. They may choose to add lines to a script, rewrite it, or create their own script. Some children will find it a comfort to stick to the prewritten script. Others will go way beyond.

Activities and Games

The activities and games allow the students to use their personas to further explore the content area. Some can be used during the discovery period or as an introduction for the unit of study. For example, in the "American Heroes for Our Times" unit, there is a scavenger hunt designed to acquaint students with biographies in the library. Other times the activities and games can be incorporated into the culminating spectacle.

Some activities use technology. In each chapter, there is at least one suggestion for how to incorporate word processing, desktop publishing, databases, CD-ROMs, or the Internet into the content area.

Displays

Displays allow students to express themselves artistically. They also help transform the library or classroom into the specific geographic area or time of the curriculum-content area.

Spectacles

Spectacles are the most elaborate of the culminating projects. These involve many or most of the students. Invite parents or the rest of the school to see and participate in the spectacles, which can be done for exhibit nights and which provide a vehicle to show the community and the rest of the school what the students have learned. They are great crowd pleasers. Consider inviting the grade just below your students so that they can get a taste of what they will learn the following year.

Conclusion

The following chapters describe in detail persona-based enrichment projects done for a particular curriculum unit of study. Each chapter provides a step-by-step guide on how to organize the persona-based enrichment project. They include a bibliography, a complete list of personas, a guide for decision making, and suggestions for culminating projects.

References

Chesler, M., and R. Fox. *Role Playing Methods in the Classroom.* Chicago: Science Research Associates, 1966.

Kimmel, M., and E. Segel. *For Reading Out Loud: A Guide to Sharing Books with Children.* New York: Delacorte Press, 1988.

Lynch-Brown, C., and C. Tomlinson. *Essentials of Children's Literature.* Boston: Allyn & Bacon, 1993.

Shaftel, F., and G. Shaftel. *Role Playing in the Curriculum.* 2d ed. Englewood Cliffs, NJ: Prentice-Hall, 1982.

Talents Unlimited. 109 South Cedar Street, Mobile, AL 36602.

Part Two

1 Camelot Alive

Introducing the
Middle Ages Through
the Legends of King Arthur

Table of Contents

The Personas of King Arthur's Court	12
Step One: Prepersona Activities	16
Step Two: Decision Making	17
Step Three: Discovery Period	20
Culminating Activities	21
A. Dramas	23
B. Activities and Games	33
C. Displays	34
D. Spectacles	38
Bibliography	41

Camelot Alive

Once upon a time, there was a place called Camelot. Arthur was king, and Guinevere was his queen. Sir Lancelot fought battles, Merlin wove magic, and the evil Mordred threatened to destroy everything. The legends of King Arthur are rich in adventure and filled with colorful characters.

Camelot was a mythological place set in the heart of the Middle Ages, which lasted 1,000 years. "Camelot Alive" combines the legend of King Arthur with the way life was in the twelfth century.

The following unit seeks to blend the reality of the period with the literature that romanticized it. Using the personas of King Arthur's court, it is hoped that students will develop a personal connection to medieval times and enjoy experiencing life in King Arthur's Middle Ages.

There is a lengthy list of activities provided in this unit. It would be impossible to do everything unless an entire school year were devoted to the subject. Start small, and choose those activities that appeal to you and your class. Start with the "Sword and the Stone" since it is the most famous of the legends. Students also enjoy creating the Big Book of Personas and taking part in a joust. These three activities allow students to experience Camelot and gain some insight into the Middle Ages.

The Personas of King Arthur's Court

The persona list identifies the main characters of King Arthur's court. The sketches are brief, and since the students will be creating a persona description, this list is only a guide and a starting place. More descriptive personas will come from the children who choose the specific characters. This list will be used with the decision-making lesson after children have been acquainted with several of the characters.

Books referring to the lesser-known characters are included in the persona list. Because these books are not indexed, some students may need to be guided to the book in which their personas exist.

> **Vortigern:** Evil Vortigern ruled Britain before Arthur was born. Vortigern's tale can be found in San Souci's *Young Merlin* and Lister's *The Legend of King Arthur*.
>
> **Aurelius:** The elder brother of Uther Pendragon who defeated the evil ruler of Britain, Vortigern. His adventure is told in Lister's *The Legend of King Arthur*.
>
> **Uther Pendragon:** This strong and passionate man was Arthur's father and king. He fell in love with his general's wife and asked Merlin for help so that he could marry her. For more details, see Lister's *The Legend of King Arthur*.
>
> **Lady Igrayne:** The beautiful, young wife of Uther Pendragon's General Gorlois. Uther could not resist the charming woman. Her tale can be found in Lister's *The Legend of King Arthur* and Perham's *King Arthur and the Legends of Camelot*.
>
> **Gorlois:** A faithful general under Uther Pendragon. He and his young wife, Igrayne, had three daughters: Margaise, Elayne, and the young Morgan le Fay. Gorlois appears in Lister's *The Legend of King Arthur*.

Margaise: The eldest daughter of Gorlois and Igrayne and the sister to the sorceress, Morgan le Fay. The evil Mordred is her son. Her tale can be found in Lister's *The Legend of King Arthur* and Morpurgo's *Arthur, High King of Britain*.

Morgan le Fay: A powerful and evil sorceress who ultimately destroys the legendary Camelot. Morgan le Fay appears in many tales, including Perham's *King Arthur and the Legends of Camelot* and Morpurgo's *Arthur, High King of Britain*.

Merlin: Perhaps the most famous magician of all time. Merlin warned Arthur not to marry Guinevere but to no avail. There are many accounts of Merlin, including San Souci's *Young Merlin*, Lister's *The Legend of King Arthur*, and Dickinson's *Merlin Dreams*.

Vivien: The ultimate femme fatale. She enticed Merlin to fall in love with her and teach her magic. The tale of Vivien is told in Bortolussi's *The Knights of the Round Table*. In some Arthurian legends, Nynyve, the Lady of the Lake, and Vivien are the same person. Because there are so few female roles, Nynyve and Vivien are considered two different individuals in this chapter.

Arthur: The once and future king who ruled Britain and created Camelot. He was the son of Uther Pendragon and Lady Igrayne. In reality, he was probably a king around the year 500. In legend, Eleanor of Aquitaine brought his stories alive for the court in the twelfth century. His ultimate downfall was his passion for Guinevere. If Arthur had taken Merlin's advice and not married Guinevere, Camelot might still exist. The adventures of Arthur are recounted from his point of view in Morpurgo's *Arthur, High King of Britain*.

Guinevere: Arthur's queen and Lancelot's true love. She was the daughter of King Leodgrance of Cameliard. As part of her dowry, she brought the Round Table to Camelot. She loved both Arthur and Lancelot but was forced to choose between them. Her early history is detailed in San Souci's *Young Guinevere*.

Sir Lancelot: The greatest of all knights, he was Arthur's beloved friend and Guinevere's beloved champion. He struggled to be loyal to his king, but his love for Guinevere proved his undoing. He and the lovely Elayne had a son named Galahad. There are many accounts of Lancelot's adventures, including Lister's *The Legend of King Arthur* and Morpurgo's *Arthur, High King of Britain*.

Lady Elayne: The daughter of King Pelles of Corbenic, her love for Lancelot was unrequited. She is the mother of Galahad. Do not confuse her with Elayne, the daughter of Igrayne and sister of Morgan le Fay. She can be found in Perham's *King Arthur and the Legends of Camelot* and Lister's *The Legend of King Arthur*, among others.

Sir Galahad: He was the son of Lancelot and Elayne and the most perfect knight. He went on the greatest quest of all: the search for the Holy Grail. Accounts of Galahad's quest can be found in Morpurgo's *Arthur, High King of Britain* and Lister's *The Legend of King Arthur*.

Nynyve, The Lady of the Lake: Sometimes called Lady Nemue, this magical woman provided Arthur with his famous sword, Excalibur. She made Arthur promise to return the sword at the end of his life. Nynyve was married to King Pelles, the Fisher King, and was a foster mother to Lancelot. There are many accounts of this tale, including Heyer's picture book *Excalibur*. There are several ladies of the lake, and some accounts consider Nynyve and Vivien to be the same person. Because there are few female roles in the Arthurian legends, they are being considered two separate individuals in this account.

King Pelles: He was also known as the Fisher King, the lord of Corbenic, and the keeper of the Holy Grail. The tale of King Pelles can be found in Lister's *The Legend of King Arthur* and Morpurgo's *Arthur, High King of Britain*. Note: *Fisher King* is a term used for the keeper of the Grail. King Pelles is one of three fisher kings.

Sir Ector: A wise and gentle knight to whom Merlin entrusted the future king, Arthur. Sir Ector had a natural-born son, Kay, but he loved the two boys equally. His story is part of Talbott's *The Sword and the Stone*.

Sir Kay: Arthur's older foster brother and eventual steward. In Morpurgo's *Arthur, High King of Britain*, he was depicted harshly, whereas most accounts portray him as simply obnoxious and self-important.

Sir Gawain: Arthur's nephew and a favorite knight of the Round Table. Gawain was hotheaded and headstrong but a loyal knight. Gawain figured prominently in Hastings's *Sir Gawain and the Green Knight* and Hastings's *Sir Gawain and the Loathly Lady*.

Lady Ragnell, The Loathly Lady: An enchantment puts the beautiful Lady Ragnell under a spell, and she becomes hideous to look at. Her wonderful story is available in Hastings's picture book, *Sir Gawain and the Loathly Lady*.

The Green Knight: Also known as Lord Bercilak, he challenged Gawain to chop his head off. His story is found in Hastings's *Sir Gawain and the Green Knight*.

Lady Bercilak: The Green Knight's wife is quite flirtatious with young Gawain. She can be found in Hastings's *Sir Gawain and the Green Knight*.

Lady-in-Waiting: In Shannon's *Gawain and the Green Knight*, young Caryn is in love with Gawain and gives him a special gift to wear.

Sir Tristram: Even this knight's name means sorrow. He is doomed never to marry his true love, Iseult. His story can be found in Morpurgo's *Arthur, High King of Britain*, Perham's *King Arthur and the Legends of Camelot*, or any of the traditional versions of the legends.

Iseult: The daughter of the Queen of Ireland, she swore vengeance on the man responsible for her brother's death. When she discovered it was Tristram, she fell in love and forgave him at once. Iseult or Isolde's tale can be found in Morpurgo's *Arthur, High King of Britain* and Perham's *King Arthur and the Legends of Camelot*.

King Marc of Cornwall: Marc was the loving uncle of Sir Tristram. He banished his nephew from his kingdom when he discovered that the young knight had fallen in love with the king's betrothed. A sympathetic account of his story can be found in Morpurgo's *Arthur, High King of Britain*.

Marhault: The giant son of the Queen of Ireland. He was a Goliath compared to Tristram's David; he was stronger, but Tristram was faster. The Cornish knight exhausted Marhault in a battle and then struck a mortal blow to his head. Look for his story in Morpurgo's *Arthur, High King of Britain*.

Sir Bedivere: Arthur's most loyal and trusting knight. His dependability was tested in the last days of Camelot. This tale can be found in Lister's *The Legend of King Arthur* and Morpurgo's *Arthur, High King of Britain*.

Sir Agravaine: This knight killed a fellow knight named Pelinore in an argument. Agravaine's adventures are told in Morpurgo's *Arthur, High King of Britain*.

The Black Knight: A powerful knight who challenged Arthur and almost won. He appears in Heyer's *Excalibur* and Hastings's *Sir Gawain and the Loathly Lady*.

Sir Gryflet: He arrived at King Arthur's court wounded by the Black Knight. His tale is found in Morpurgo's *Arthur, High King of Britain*.

Sir Percival: He was the son of the murdered Pelinore and a member of the second generation of knights which included Galahad and Mordred.

Sir Gaheris: This knight remained loyal to King Arthur and was killed by Lancelot. After he died, his brother, Gawain, swore revenge and would not rest until he and Arthur battled Lancelot. This tale can be found in Lister's *The Legend of King Arthur*.

Sir Bors: When Camelot was divided between Arthur and Lancelot, Bors joined his cousin, Lancelot. He was in a position to kill King Arthur, but Lancelot would not allow it. His contributions are contained in Morpurgo's *Arthur, High King of Britain*.

Sir Gareth: He came to Camelot disguised as a peasant but proved himself to be a fearless fighter. His story is recounted in Hodges's *The Kitchen Knight* and Perham's *King Arthur and the Legends of Camelot*.

Lady Linette: This fair maiden came to Camelot in search of a champion for her sister, Lady Linesse. Much to her dismay, a mere kitchen boy was dispatched to aid her. Her tale is part of Hodges's *The Kitchen Knight*.

Lady Linesse: She was the quintessential damsel in distress. She was locked in a castle tower by the cruel Red Knight. Her champion turned out to be Sir Gareth of Orkney, and the two of them fell in love. Their tale is told in Hodges's *The Kitchen Knight*.

Red Knight: One of the most powerful and tyrannical brutes to fight one of the knights of the Round Table. He imprisoned the fair Lady Linesse in his castle. His adventure is told in Hodges's *The Kitchen Knight*.

Mordred: Arthur's evil "nephew" and the ultimate downfall of Camelot. His tale is told in Lister's *The Legend of King Arthur*, Perham's *King Arthur and the Legends of King Arthur*, and Morpurgo's *Arthur, High King of Britain*.

Mother Hild: An old nun who cared for Merlin as a young boy. Her tale is part of San Souci's *Young Merlin*.

Archbishop of Canterbury: He presided over the contest of the Sword and the Stone. He is a prominent character in Talbott's *The Sword in the Stone*.

Eleanor of Aquitaine: Not a member of Arthur's court, this real queen was fond of the Arthurian legends and the code of courtly love and made the legends fashionable. She and her husband, Henry II, searched for the grave of Arthur and believed they discovered it.

Note: There is not much variety in female characters in the legends of Arthur. For this reason, girls should be encouraged to take boys' parts. When a large number of children are participating, students can create personas of monks, nuns, villains, peasants, shopkeepers, and a town crier. Guidelines for creating a unique character are part of the "Who Am I?" handout.

Step One: Prepersona Activities

1. Read several stories to introduce children to some of the characters of Camelot. Be sure to include tales that introduce the lesser-known characters.
   Some great books to read aloud are Talbott's *The Sword and the Stone*, Heyer's *Excalibur*, Service's *The Wizard of Wind and Rock*, Shannon's *Gawain and the Green Knight*, Hastings's *Sir Gawain and the Loathly Lady*, and Hodges's *The Kitchen Knight* plus selected chapters from Morpurgo's *Arthur, High King of Britain* and Perham's *King Arthur and the Legends of Camelot*. See the bibliography for further information.

2. Introduce the Middle Ages. Persona-based enrichment provides many avenues for learning about the Middle Ages; however, you may want to provide some background. Topics that might be covered are feudalism, guilds, the Black Death, the church in medieval society, and castle life. These topics are also explored in the persona-based enrichment projects.

3. Develop strategies to introduce children to role playing: Read Talbott's story of *The Sword in the Stone*, an excellent story to read aloud. Have children reenact the story by role-playing the characters of Sir Ector, Arthur, Kay, and Merlin. (Although Arthur's mother, Igrayne, only appears at the beginning, her point of view is interesting to explore.) A skit of this story is included in this chapter.

To encourage children to start thinking in the first person, ask them the following questions. Responses may be written or oral.

A. What if you were Arthur? How would you feel about being king? What would be the first thing you would do?

B. What if you were a townsperson? How would you feel if you were a grown-up at the tournament, and the only person who could pull the sword from the stone was a teenage boy? Would you want a young boy as your king?

C. What if you were Kay? How would you feel about your little brother becoming the ruler of the kingdom?

Step Two: Decision Making

When students have been introduced to some of the stories and they begin to acquire a working knowledge of some of the relationships of the characters in Camelot, the persona element can be introduced.

1. Explain to students that they will be choosing a persona and will be doing projects as that person. Talk about some of the culminating projects. Explain that there are many different types of projects and that each child will be taking part in several projects. Explain that some of the well-known personas, such as King Arthur, will probably be in a performance. If students wish to be in a performance, they should choose a well-known character. If they wish to concentrate on a different kind of project, they may pick some of the lesser-known personas.

2. Each student will be asked to make three choices. They will be asked to give reasons why they chose this character. Their reasons will be important if two or more children want to be the same persona.

3. Place a copy of the Camelot criteria for decision making (see pp. 18-19) in a visible place. Encourage students to invent additional criteria.

4. Review the list of personas, and emphasize the lesser-known characters. Allow students to refer to the list of the personas when making their choices.

5. Explain that, in addition to specific personas, a student can opt to create a persona. For example, if a student wishes, he may make up a knight, creating a name and a whole range of adventures. A student can choose a knight, nobility, magician, evil knight, serf, shopkeeper, or peasant.

6. Have students complete the King Arthur decision-making work sheet.

7. Meet with each student individually. Students should be happy and comfortable with their choices.

Name _____

CAMELOT DECISION-MAKING WORK SHEET

DECISION: WHICH PERSONA DO I WANT TO BECOME FOR THE FAIR?

Below is a list of alternatives:

> KNIGHTS: Agravaine, Bedivere, Bors, Ector, Gaheris, Galahad, Gareth, Gawain, Gryflet, Kay, Lancelot, Percival, Tristram

> NOBILITY: Elayne, Iseult, Lady Bercilak, Lady Igrayne, Lady Linette, Lady Ragnell, Linesse, Margaise

> ROYALTY: Eleanor of Aquitaine, King Arthur, King Marc, King Pelles, Queen Guinevere, Uther Pendragon

> MAGICIANS: Morgan le Fay, Merlin, Nynyve, Vivien

> EVIL KNIGHTS: Black Knight, Green Knight, Red Knight, Marhault, Mordred, Vortigern

> CLERGY: Archbishop of Canterbury, Mother Hild, monks and nuns

> VILLAINS: court jesters, peasants, serfs, shopkeepers, town criers

Answer the questions on the following page. Use your answers to help you make a decision concerning your persona. Give several reasons for your decision.

Give three alternative personas in order of preference.

1. _____

2. _____

3. _____

From The Persona Book. © 1997. Katherine Lallier and Nancy Marino. TIP. (800) 237-6124.

Name _____

CAMELOT DECISION-MAKING WORK SHEET
Page 2

DECISION: WHICH PERSONA DO I WANT TO BECOME FOR THE FAIR?

Criteria:

1. Why do I want to be this persona?

2. What do I like about the persona of the character?

3. Do I want to have a big part in the performance?

4. Will I do extra research concerning this character?

5. Will I be able to design and make the costume?

Step Three: Discovery Period

During this time, students delve into the Middle Ages. Although they should be encouraged to collect information about their persona, the primary purpose of this unit is to explore the Middle Ages. Library time is discovery time. Students examine books, CD-ROMs, encyclopedias, and other sources for information about the Middle Ages. Every classroom lesson gives students more information about how their personas lived and behaved. Students can create persona journals. These journals, written in the first person, can include answers to questions.

Where did I live? (a castle, cottage)

What did I like to eat?

What was my status in medieval society?

What did I do for fun?

What was a typical day like?

What did I wear?

What dangers did I face?

IMPORTANT NOTE: While students can glean personality traits about their persona from reading the literature, the answers to most of the above questions are not found in the legends of Camelot. (For example, there are no books that tell the favorite food of King Arthur or Guinevere. At the same time, no one can claim pizza as their favorite food in medieval England.) Therefore, students will have to apply what they learn about the Middle Ages. Teachers may want to plan activities that help students better understand that time period; for example, students could be served a medieval meal, or parents could be asked to allow students to sleep on the floor in a cold room so that students can better understand what it was like to live in a castle.

Personas may report on various topics. Below is a list of topics that certain types of personas may wish to pursue:

Knights (Lancelot, Gawain, etc.) and Evil Knights (Mordred, etc.)
    Weaponry   The Hundred Years' War
    Crusades

Nobility (Lady Igrayne, Lady Linette, etc.) and Royalty (King Arthur, etc.)
    Castles   Falconry
    Heraldry

Magicians (Merlin, Morgan le Fay, Nynyve, etc.)
    Medieval medicine
    Entertainment and magic

Clergy (Monks and Nuns)
  Religion in medieval times
  Printing and illuminated manuscripts

Villains (Serfs, Town Crier, Shopkeepers, Peasants)
  Feudalism   Guilds
  The Black Death

Students may work in groups or separately. Each group could report to the class about their chosen topic.

Who Am I?

The "Who Am I?" work sheet (see page 22) encourages students to create a page for the Big Book of Personas. This is one of the important culminating activities. Writing is one of the most difficult tasks that students are asked to do. Any adult would agree that a blank piece of paper is quite intimidating especially in regard to creative writing. This questionnaire is provided to ease students into the writing process. The results, written in the first person, will be included on their page of "King Arthur's Big Book of Personas." The children will also design a picture of their personas to accompany the creative writing.

Culminating Activities

A medieval fair or a theater-in-the-round production are exciting activities for your knights, serfs, and nobility. The theater-in-the-round allows students to tell their persona's story. The medieval fair is a collection of displays, demonstrations, spectacles, and games that center on Arthurian lore.

Below are the types of culminating activities for this unit. Select a limited number of activities.

Dramas. Choose dramas if you and your students wish to perform a theater-in-the-round play. The skits on the following pages provide a basic outline. Have your students enhance these skits or create their own.

Activities and Games. These are interactive games and activities that can be prepared for a medieval fair. Even the preparation is a learning process. For example, students can design a castle that is true to the architecture of that time for the game "Capture Mordred's Knights." Allow the student playing Mordred to run the game, and encourage guests to ask him about his persona.

Displays. The displays and demonstrations are perfect ways to transform your classroom, library, or school gym into a place from the Middle Ages.

Spectacles. Spectacles are activities that are performed in front of an audience. They differ from dramas inasmuch as many students may participate in these activities. They are always audience favorites.

Student's Name _____

Persona's Name _____

CAMELOT WHO AM I? WORK SHEET

Whether your persona comes from the Arthurian legends or is a character you are creating, you must let everyone know who you are. In no fewer than five sentences, tell me who you are.

Examples of what you might include are:

1. What is your job?

2. If you are a monk, shopkeeper, or knight, why did you become that?

3. Are you related to anyone in Camelot?

4. Whether your character is legendary or created, did you have an interesting adventure? (If not, make one up!)

5. Do you know how your life will end? Do tell.

6. Some of you—especially monks, nuns, and peasants—might have a secret that no one knows. Care to tell?

7. Describe yourself—brave, shy, mysterious, obnoxious, arrogant, clever, romantic, beautiful, loyal, dedicated, feisty, fiendish, fair, ferocious, humble, honor-bound, chivalrous, cold-blooded, honest, powerful, charismatic, smart, curious?

From *The Persona Book*. © 1997. Katherine Lallier and Nancy Marino. TIP. (800) 237-6124.

A. Dramas

The following are a collection of performance scripts based on the legends of King Arthur. The minimal dialogue allows students to make additions. They might also expand or create their own dramas. Keep stage instructions to a minimum, and encourage students to role-play. The dramas also reflect actual customs of the Middle Ages, such as the knighting ceremony.

One of the most famous of all the Arthurian legends is "The Sword in the Stone." This skit can be included in any Camelot production either as a performance, a puppet show, or some other method of your own design. After students have researched their personas and the time period, introduce the scripts.

"The Sword in the Stone"

Characters:
Arthur   Kay   Sir Ector
Archbishop   Merlin

Scene: Near the courtyard where the sword in the stone is in view.

ARCHBISHOP: Merlin, I'm worried. Since the death of good King Uther Pendragon, Britain has been in a state of war. The people are downhearted, and I have no idea how to cheer them up. Without a strong king to lead us, I fear for our country's survival.

MERLIN: Fear not, your Excellency. I have a solution. If you will allow me to use my magic, I will create a contest, the likes of which have never been seen.

ARCHBISHOP: What are you planning, Merlin?

MERLIN: You will soon see. You will soon see.

(Exit Archbishop and Merlin. Enter Kay and Arthur.)

KAY: Finally I get to prove myself as the great knight I know I will be at this tournament. Arthur, fetch me my sword.

ARTHUR: Okay. Where is your sword, Kay?

KAY: You are my squire, brother. You should know where my sword is. Don't tell me you've misplaced it—I'll have your head!

ARTHUR: Kay, I was only teasing. Would I lose my brother's sword? I'll fetch it for you now. *(Arthur runs off as Kay practices for the tournament.)*

From *The Persona Book.* © 1997. Katherine Lallier and Nancy Marino. TIP. (800) 237-6124.

KAY: And be quick!

ARTHUR: Oh, no. My brother is about to fight in his first tournament, and I have lost his sword. What kind of good-for-nothing squire am I?

Wait a minute. Didn't I see a sword stuck in a stone outside the old church? I'll just borrow that one and return it when Kay is done with it. No one will be the wiser. *(Arthur walks over to the sword in the stone.)*

Funny, I thought there were guards here. I guess they took off for the tournament too. *(Arthur gets the sword and takes it to Kay.)*

KAY: *(Takes the sword for his own.)* Arthur, where did you get this?

(Enter Sir Ector)

SIR ECTOR: Kay, where did you get that sword?

KAY: It's mine, Father! I have the sword from the stone! That makes me England's next king!

SIR ECTOR: I repeat, my son, where did you get this sword?

KAY: Arthur brought it to me, but. . .

SIR ECTOR: Arthur, my boy, how did you get this sword from the stone?

ARTHUR: I simply pulled it out like this.

(Sir Ector and Kay kneel to Arthur.)

ARTHUR: Get up, Father. What are you doing?

SIR ECTOR: Arthur, I have loved you like my own dear son, but you are not my own. You are the son of the great King Uther Pendragon and the rightful king of Britain.

(Enter Merlin)

MERLIN: It is true, Arthur. When you were a baby, I brought you to Sir Ector to protect you from your father's enemies. You are now ready to take your place in history, and I shall be at your side as your counselor and friend.

ALL: Long live King Arthur! Long live the king!

From *The Persona Book.* © 1997. Katherine Lallier and Nancy Marino. TIP. (800) 237-6124.

The Making of a Knight

"The Making of a Knight" was created by a librarian with the assistance of two students who chose the personas of Lancelot and Galahad. They researched the authentic steps a squire took to become a knight, but literary license was used to include Lady Elayne in the ceremony. The tone of this drama is serious and sacred. During the Middle Ages the church was a powerful force, dictating almost every facet of life. For this reason, this knighting ceremony has many religious elements. However, they can be modified to a teacher's particular needs.

Characters:
Arthur   Galahad   Town Crier
Elayne   Lancelot

Scene: The chapel. Few sets and props are required. A white sheet or tablecloth thrown over a table to signify an altar is needed. An ornamental dish or goblet and a pair of candlesticks will add a sacred tone. A bowl with water to represent the knight's purifying bath can be included. Finally, a white tunic, a scarlet cloak, and black shoes and stockings as well as the knight's spurs, armor, and weapons need to be placed on the altar. King Arthur will need his sword, Excalibur.

TOWN CRIER: Hear ye, hear ye! Come one, come all, to see the dubbing of Sir Galahad.

ARTHUR: It has been foretold that the greatest knight who will ever walk the Earth would fill the Siege Perilous. Any man not worthy who attempted to sit in it would immediately perish from this Earth. When your father, Sir Lancelot, came to Camelot, I thought the "Perilous Seat" was meant for him. But it was not to be. It has remained empty for so long that I had almost given up hope of ever meeting the man who was worthy enough to sit in it. It pleases me greatly that it was meant for you, Galahad.

ELAYNE: Your father and I are so proud to bear witness to your becoming a knight of the Round Table. Each of us knows in our heart that you will be successful in your quest for the Holy Grail.

ARTHUR: Galahad, prepare yourself for the noble duty of being dubbed a knight of the Round Table.

LANCELOT: *(Lancelot explains the steps as Galahad acts them out.)* The first step in becoming a knight happened last night. The squire enters the chapel and prays. He prays that he is worthy of becoming a knight. Next, he washes. This act symbolizes the act of becoming pure. Sometimes the knight cuts a lock of hair or even shaves his face and head as a sign that he honors God.

Galahad is wearing special clothes for this solemn event. Each piece has a special meaning. The white tunic he wears means that he is pure in spirit. Over his tunic he places a scarlet cloak as a sign that he is willing to shed his blood in battle. Finally, his shoes and stockings are black to show that he is not afraid to die.

Since last night, Galahad has been fasting, but his hunger will know an end. There will be a great celebration after the king dubs my son. There will be feasting and dancing as well as the opportunity for the new knight to show off his riding skills and use of weaponry. But more importantly, Galahad will know no hunger of spirit for he will be a knight of the Round Table.

(King Arthur ties the sword around Galahad.)

King Arthur will now perform the ceremony of girding the armor. He has belted Galahad's sword to his waist and provided him with his spurs and shield.

ARTHUR: Are you prepared to take your solemn vows?

GALAHAD: I am, my lord.

ARTHUR: As a knight of the Round Table, you are bound to be brave and honorable, to serve God and your king, to fight for what is right, to protect the weak, to honor women—all in the name of chivalry.

GALAHAD: I will, my lord.

(Galahad kneels before King Arthur.)

ARTHUR: In the name of St. George* and St. Michael,** I dub thee a knight of the Round Table. *(Holds sword over head.)* Be brave, ready, and loyal. *(Arthur buffets† Galahad.)* Godspeed, Sir Galahad.

---

*St. George the dragon slayer is the patron saint of England.
**St. Michael is the archangel who led an army of angels to banish Lucifer from heaven.
†Buffet: An openhanded slap to the cheek.

From *The Persona Book.* © 1997. Katherine Lallier and Nancy Marino. TIP. (800) 237-6124.

Two Tales of Sir Gawain

Sir Gawain is the epitome of impetuous youth. His stories are wonderful examples of the expression Look Before You Leap.

Characters:
Dame Ragnell, the Loathly Lady *Lady-in-Waiting*
Green Knight *Sir Gawain*
Lady Bercilak

Sir Gawain, the brave. [Portrayed by Joey Gallagher.]

GAWAIN: My lords and ladies of the kingdom of_____ _____ *(your school name or class teacher's name)*, let me present myself. I am Sir Gawain, a knight of King Arthur's famous Round Table. I have many adventures of which I am proud. But the two I am going to share with you now show what happens if you don't look before you leap. One year around Yuletide, the knights of the Round Table were telling of their many quests and adventures. I was a young knight, so I did not have many adventures under my belt . . . yet.

From *The Persona Book*. © 1997. Katherine Lallier and Nancy Marino. TIP. (800) 237-6124.

LADY-IN-WAITING: Pardon me, Sir Gawain, but let me tell what happened that night.

GAWAIN: Certainly, m'lady.

LADY-IN-WAITING: The knights were teasing shy Sir Gawain terribly. They made fun of his youth and the fact that he had not yet been on a quest. The lords and ladies all laughed at him, and I wanted to cry. But suddenly, a great booming voice filled the castle.

GREEN KNIGHT: Brave and noble knights—or so they say you are. I would like to test your courage in the form of a game. Which one of you will take my ax and strike a blow to my neck? I will not fight you if that is what you fear. I will simply lay my head down, and you may sever it from my neck. If I do manage to survive this decapitation, I ask one tiny favor. You simply have to allow me to swing the ax at you in return. It is only fair. However, I will not attempt to chop your head off until a year and a day from today. Any takers?

GAWAIN: Me! Me! I will do it! I accept your challenge, Green Knight. (*To audience*) After all, the odds seemed to be in my favor. How could he possibly survive an ax blow? I may have had few adventures, but I certainly could wield an ax. What could possibly go wrong?

LADY-IN-WAITING: Well, something went terribly wrong. No one could believe their eyes.

(*Green Knight kneels down to accept the ax blow.*)

GREEN KNIGHT: Good luck, Sir Gawain! Ready when you are!

(*Gawain chops the knight's head off.*)

GAWAIN: Oh, my.

(*Green Knight retrieves his head.*)

GREEN KNIGHT: And now, Sir Gawain, I bid you farewell. I will see you at the Green Chapel in one year's time. Enjoy the time you have left. (*Exits, laughing*)

From *The Persona Book*. © 1997. Katherine Lallier and Nancy Marino. TIP. (800) 237-6124.

A. Dramas: Two Tales of Sir Gawain   29

LADY-IN-WAITING: Gawain was true to his word, and in one year's time he set off on his horse, Gringolet, to find the Green Knight's chapel. I gave him a small gift of my affection: a sash I had made to give him luck on his journey.

GAWAIN: Thank-you, dear lady. I will never take it off. And I will return, you know.

LADY-IN-WAITING: Good-bye, Gawain. Fare-thee-well. (*Exits*)

LADY BERCILAK: Gawain traveled many weeks before he arrived at the castle of my husband, Lord Bercilak. I welcomed the young knight and insisted he stay for a Yuletide feast. (*To Gawain*) Rest here for the night, Sir Gawain. I will take you to the Green Chapel in plenty of time to meet your date with destiny.

GAWAIN: You are too kind, Lady Bercilak. If this is to be my last evening on Earth, it is my great pleasure to spend it with you.

LADY BERCILAK: You are a most chivalrous knight. Would you dance with me, Sir Gawain?

GAWAIN: I do not think I should, my lady.

LADY BERCILAK: Nonsense. You will not be betraying your dear lady-in-waiting with one little dance. And I have a secret to tell you, so now you must dance with me.

(*They dance.*)

LADY BERCILAK: The Green Knight will surely sever your head tomorrow, but I know a way you might be spared. Give me your sash in exchange for this one. This is a magical sash that will protect you from the Green Knight's deadly ax.

GAWAIN: Your offer is kind. But if I do indeed lose my life, it will be with the sash I now wear. I made a promise.

LADY BERCILAK: So be it then. Good luck, Sir Gawain. You will need it. (*Exits*)

GREEN KNIGHT: The next day, Gawain kept his date with destiny. As I sharpened my ax, I heard him approach. (*To Gawain*) Welcome, lad!

From *The Persona Book.* © 1997. Katherine Lallier and Nancy Marino. TIP. (800) 237-6124.

GAWAIN:	I am ready to keep my promise to you. *(Gawain kneels before the Green Knight. The Green Knight strikes a blow, but only a trickle of blood comes from Gawain's neck.)*
GAWAIN:	You did not chop my head off. Why not?
GREEN KNIGHT:	Consider yourself a true champion in our little game! You proved your knightly virtues when you accepted our challenge and your honesty and courage when you met me today. But most important of all, you were true to your own heart.
LADY-IN-WAITING:	Gawain returned to me, but he was not mine for long. Another adventure even more splendid than this awaited the young knight.
GAWAIN:	If you thought that adventure put me in the middle of things, listen while I tell you what I volunteered for next. King Arthur needed a champion, or he would have to forfeit his life to the Black Knight. The only way he could save himself and his kingdom was to answer the Black Knight's riddle. I, of course, volunteered to help him. But Dame Ragnell can explain this tale better than I.
DAME RAGNELL:	I may be hideous to look at, but listen to me carefully and you will understand why. King Arthur searched the land looking for someone who could answer the Black Knight's riddle: What do women most desire? Unfortunately, every woman he asked gave him a different answer. And then he met me.
GREEN KNIGHT:	Although this adventure does not include us, we must describe this lady's hideous looks. Her nose was bulbous and pimply.
LADY BERCILAK:	What teeth she had were large, yellow, and crusted.
LADY-IN-WAITING:	Her face was covered with popping pustules.
GREEN KNIGHT:	And she was a hunchback.
LADY BERCILAK:	She was the ugliest thing anyone has ever set their eyes on. She was a truly loathly lady.
DAME RAGNELL:	Come on, guys, I am not that ugly.

From *The Persona Book.* © 1997. Katherine Lallier and Nancy Marino. TIP. (800) 237-6124.

A. Dramas: Two Tales of Sir Gawain

GREEN KNIGHT,
LADY BERCILAK,
LADY-IN-WAITING: Wanna bet?

DAME RAGNELL: I knew the answer to the Black Knight's riddle, and I whispered it to King Arthur. But in return, I asked one small favor. I asked that one of the knights of the Round Table become my husband.

GAWAIN: This is where I fit in. King Arthur told us knights of a lady who answered the Black Knight's question and thereby saved the kingdom. But he owed her a favor. I volunteered then and there. Then he told me I would have to marry the Loathly Lady. My advice to all of you out there is to get all the facts before you volunteer for anything. Of course, I had made a promise, so I had to keep it.

DAME RAGNELL: When I saw that it was Gawain, I felt lucky indeed. He fell to his knee and asked. . .

GAWAIN: Will you marry me, my lady?

DAME RAGNELL: They brought me back to Camelot for the marriage. The way everybody acted though, it seemed more like a funeral. I know I'm not exactly beautiful, but looks are not everything, you know.

GAWAIN: The most amazing thing happened after everyone had gone home. There before me stood not the Loathly Lady but the most beautiful maiden I had ever seen. I asked where my wife was, and she said. . .

DAME RAGNELL: Do you not recognize me, Gawain? I am Dame Ragnell. I am the Loathly Lady. I was under an enchantment. Because you married me, you broke half the spell. For half the day, I will be beautiful, as you see me now. But for the rest of the time, I will return to my disgusting, loathly shape. If you can answer one question correctly, you will break the rest of the spell, and I can always look like this. Would you rather have me hideous by day or by night?

GAWAIN: If I have to choose, I suppose I would rather have you beautiful by night.

From *The Persona Book*. © 1997. Katherine Lallier and Nancy Marino. TIP. (800) 237-6124.

Sir Gawain and Dame Ragnell, the Loathly Lady. [Left to right, Joey Gallagher and Kristyn Boccia.]

DAME RAGNELL: That is very cruel of you. You would have me looking ugly during the day in front of all your friends so they can laugh at me?

GAWAIN: I'm sorry. That was thoughtless. Be beautiful by day.

DAME RAGNELL: Well, you must not love me very much if you would want to look at me all night long in my ugly state.

GAWAIN: No, no. I do love you, but I do not know what to choose for you. Ragnell, you must choose for yourself, and that is the decision I will live with.

DAME RAGNELL: Oh, my husband, you did it! That's the right answer! You have given me what every woman most desires: to decide for herself.

GAWAIN: As it turns out, that was the answer that the Loathly Lady whispered to King Arthur. Every person wants to make his or her own decisions. I was happy that that adventure turned out so well.

From *The Persona Book*. © 1997. Katherine Lallier and Nancy Marino. TIP. (800) 237-6124.

LADY BERCILAK:	And so ends the tale of Sir Gawain and the Loathly Lady.
GREEN KNIGHT:	But fear not, there are many other adventures starring Gawain and the other knights of the Round Table.
LADY-IN-WAITING:	All you need to do to find out about them is to pick up a book at the library.

From *The Persona Book*. © 1997. Katherine Lallier and Nancy Marino. TIP. (800) 237-6124.

B. Activities and Games

In a traditional medieval fair, there are always games and interactive entertainment for the audience. Give it an Arthurian twist with some of the following activities.

Galahad's Quest for the Fisher King: A Maze

In this activity, Galahad invites audience participants to enter a maze to search for King Pelles, also known as the Fisher King and the keeper of the Holy Grail. The maze might be decorated with perils such as the evil Black Knight or a fire-breathing dragon. The Fisher King waits at the end of the maze holding a goblet filled with candy fish or goldfish crackers. This activity is so simple yet highly entertaining to younger lords and ladies. The prize of a small scroll or the "fish" treat has always been well received.

How to Build the Maze: Several stanchions are required to build the frame of the maze. Fishing wire or strong cord is tied from stanchion to stanchion, and mural paper hangs down to create the walls. The mural paper needs to be sealed shut between panels with tape and affixed to the floor. The design of the maze does not have to be intricate. A simple *u* or *s* shape is entertaining, especially if the mural paper has been decorated with scenes from the Castle Corbenic.

King Arthur Knights the Commoners: An Obstacle Course

This activity is perhaps the most exciting part of the fair. King Arthur's knights have created an obstacle course for the serfs and villains of Camelot. Using a toy lance, the commoner must knock balls off road cones. The next task is to step through tires and crawl through a tunnel. The obstacles can be a combination of whatever you have readily available. At the end of the course, the commoner kneels before King Arthur, who uses his sword to knight the young serf. "In the name of St. Michael and St. George, I dub thee a knight of the Round Table. Be brave, ready, and loyal." The new knight or lady may wear a shield or helmet during the ceremony or receive a certificate announcing his or her knighthood. The course can be made a little more difficult if the knight-to-be must "ride" a stick pony, but note that he or she will lose the use of one hand by having to carry the pony. Older children enjoy this simple obstacle course as well if one adds a modern-day stopwatch and times the worthy squires. Several knights need to be stationed at this activity so that it can be put back together quickly for the next challenger. Younger squires will enjoy being "sponsored" or helped by knights of the Round Table—a common tradition in medieval times.

Games for the Fair

The following activities can be set up at gaming booths. To give ordinary tables a festive look, collect wrapping-paper tubes. Decorate the tubes with crepe paper and tape it to the tabletops. (You will need one on each side of the table.) Once the "poles" are firmly fixed to the tables, use a twisted crepe-paper streamer between the two poles. For a fancier look, flags can be taped to the top of the wrapping-paper tube.

Capture Mordred's Knights: The evil Mordred must be stopped by catapulting beanbags through the castle portcullis (castle gate). Design a castle front from a sturdy piece of cardboard, Styrofoam, or plywood. Include windows and a portcullis as targets through which the bean bags may be thrown. Award the winners flags to use at the upcoming joust.

The Sword in the Stone: Toss the ring on the sword in the stone, and maybe you were meant to be the king of Britain. The sword in the stone is a simple design. Wrap a medium-sized box in aluminum foil. Mold the edges to resemble an anvil. Glue a piece of oaktag to the front declaring, Whosoever Pulleth This Sword from This Stone Is Rightwise Born King of England. Cut a slit in the top of the box, and insert a toy sword. Use rings from a ring-toss game or Frisbee rings to throw at the mounted sword. Award the winners flags to use at the upcoming joust. (Flags can be made by tying a piece of crepe paper to a small stick.)

C. Displays

The following offers students the opportunity to express their knowledge of the Middle Ages creatively.

The Wedding Feast of Uther Pendragon to Lady Igrayne

Cover a long table with a white tablecloth. One of the important items on a medieval table is "the salt." Cover a bowl with aluminum foil for the salt dispenser. It had great significance because those who sat "above the salt" enjoyed a higher social status than those who sat below. Other essential elements are drinking goblets or tankards as well as spoons and a few knives. Forks were not fashionable in England at the time, and most people carried their own knives. Fingers were the popular utensil of the period. A person called a ewerer would pour water on the guests' hands between courses. There were no individual place settings. Platters were shared between guests. Food was served on trenchers, which were large squares of stale bread that would soak up juices and gravy.

Food can either be real or papier-mâché models of medieval delicacies. For inspiration for a papier-mâché feast, look to Aliki's *A Medieval Feast* for wonderful pictures of the period. Actual recipes are included in Cosman's *Fabulous Feasts*.

A medieval table.

Students can use the table for the performance of Uther and Igrayne's wedding. Besides Uther and Igrayne and their wedding guests, include a butler, ewerer, panter, usher, and chamberlain. The *butler* was in charge of wine only. The *ewerer* gave the guests water to clean their hands. The *panter* was the guardian of the bread, and the *usher* served the food. The job of *chamberlain* was extremely important: He or she would taste the food to make sure it was not poisoned.

If the table is not used during a performance, it can still provide a vivid display for the medieval fair. Children can create cards to explain the objects and their importance at the table. If the table is a display for the medieval fair, then by creating a "blackbird pie" students become more involved in the project because they have to guess how many blackbirds—or marbles or anything—are baked inside. A small token of Uther and Igrayne's esteem awaits the lord or lady with the best estimate.

Subtlety

One gastronomical project that can be created is a subtlety or soteltes. These were sweets and jellies molded into shapes, such as lions, crowns, or eagles. At times these large, edible sugary sculptures were elaborate—depicting anything from a knight's deeds to a nature scene. Students can create their own subtlety. Start with sugar cubes and icing. Then add licorice sticks, chocolate wafers, peppermint swirls, or any other type of candy.

Sir Lancelot's Personal Quintain

As simple to build as a wooden scarecrow, a quintain helped knights prepare for tournaments and battle. The knight would try to strike the shield held by the quintain. If he was not quick, he would surely be unhorsed by the sandbag also held by the wooden knight. An old coatrack or a wooden pole with a crosspiece nailed on is the perfect skeleton for the quintain. A shield must be hung on one side and a stuffed pillowcase on the other. Because this is only a display item, it need not swivel. See Hunt's *Illuminations* for a picture of a quintain.

King Arthur's Castle Contest

Cooperative groups of students can design castles and compete for best portcullis, drawbridge, turret, castle keep, and other architectural wonders. The element of competition has been included, but each castle can win a ribbon if the awards are for a specific piece of architecture, such as the bailey, moat, or gatehouse. Materials needed include a multitude of boxes in varying sizes and plenty of gray and black paint. No doubt the student architects will provide their own props and materials to make their castle unique. Students should create their castles on paper first to ensure that all the basic elements are there. There are many excellent books on castles, including Macaulay's *Castle*, Platt's *Stephen Biesty's Cross Sections: Castles,* and *A Medieval Castle* by MacDonald and Bergin. Ultimately, students should design their own version of Arthur's fabled Camelot.

A high-tech variation on this project is to use *Kid CAD* by Davidson Inc., run on Windows. This software program allows students to create all kinds of architectural structures, including castles in a three-dimensional format.

Big Book of Personas/Royal Portrait Gallery

The Big Book of Personas is a bound collection of the students' characters. Before its contents are made into a book, however, the pages should decorate the classroom walls, allowing visitors to get to know the people behind the Arthurian legends. Students need to research medieval costumes and armor to design their characters accurately. Some students may choose to draw a full-body picture, and others may style the picture more like a portrait. Still others may draw a scene from an adventure. The choice belongs to the children. Using stencils for the personas' names will add uniformity to the pictures in the gallery, as will using drawing sheets of the same size—possibly 18 by 24 inches. Students should use the "Who Am I?" sheet in this chapter to write a synopsis of their character in the first person. After the drawing, stenciling, and the persona synopses are complete, have the children color the background with pastel chalk. This technique brings out the drawing and adds another bit of uniformity. If possible, laminate the finished work for durability, and bind the pages. It is now the Big Book of Personas.

C. Displays 37

Court Jesters and Town Criers

Encourage a few children to create a persona for a jester or town crier. Juggling scarves is quite flamboyant and still a relatively easy skill for the jester to master. (Because the chiffon scarves flow slowly through the air, they are easy to catch, and their bright, flowing colors are impressive.) Court jesters can also be used for face painting if you wish to add a carnival element to your fair. For more information about jesters, read Fradon's *The King's Fool: A Book About Medieval and Renaissance Fools*.

Town criers can take the part of masters of ceremonies. They announce the beginning and ending of activities and keep the festivities moving. Using a bell and a scroll, town criers can wander through the crowds with important announcements or introduce the next segment of the fair.

Court jesters and town criers lend a festive air to the world of Camelot.

Camelot's Portcullis

The portcullis is the spiked gate that could be raised and lowered in the castle. If your fair is held indoors, it is a simple and effective decoration. It can be used as an entrance to your classroom, library, gym, or auditorium. Cut strips of black construction paper so that they are large enough to fit the width of the doorway and long enough to cover the top third of the entranceway. Glue them together to form a grid. Cut points on the strips that face downward to create spikes. Attach these to the door, hanging them low enough so that people have to duck to enter the room. The audience will immediately have the feeling they have stepped into a castle from long ago.

D. Spectacles

The next three activities are favorites for audience members and participants. Each is a spectacle that brings "ahs" from the toughest audiences.

The Maypole Dance

The Maypole is a traditional folk dance that was quite popular during the Middle Ages. Because the dance is precise, it requires rehearsal and students who follow directions well. The end result is a beautifully braided Maypole. Ask your physical-education teacher to explain the dance, or look in a book with traditional dances.

The pole or stanchion needs to be at least 7 feet high. If one is available, use a volleyball pole with wheels so that it is mobile. Twelve sturdy ribbons are needed, one for each dancer. Use plastic Chinese ribbons, which are available in most physical-education catalogs. Affix one end of the ribbon to a ruler, and then tape the ruler to the inside of a hollow volleyball pole.

The Live Chess Game

In many of the adult renditions of the Camelot tales, chess plays an important role. Some say that Sir Tristram and Iseult fell in love over a game of chess. In another version, King Marc of Cornwall—Tristram's uncle and the fiancé of Iseult—was playing chess when he learned of their betrayal. Chess was a popular game in the Middle Ages and was enjoyed by royalty.

To create a live chess game, create a chess board out of two colors of mural paper. Make sure it is large enough for students to act as the chess pieces. Before the pieces take their place on the board, they can explain their function in medieval society as well as in the game. The description of the anthropomorphic chess pieces is included in Kidder's *Illustrated Chess for Children*.

Start the game midway, with no more than 20 moves until checkmate. Use only 10 to 12 chess pieces to avoid overcrowding and confusion. Ask a child who is interested in chess to design the end of a game. When pieces are captured, let the students act out their demise on the board. The audience loves it, and the students are able to learn many of the principles of chess. Chess is a great activity for logical, mathematical thinkers, and the live chess game gives them an opportunity to excel.

A sample chess game follows. Every piece, or child, on the board has an opportunity to either move, capture another piece, or be captured. Although such a game is not based on sound chess principles—at one point, for example, instead of saving his king, a bishop runs away—it does show how each major piece moves. That bishop running demonstrates the diagonal movement of that particular piece.

Key:

W = white — means moves to   N = knight
B = black x means captures   B = bishop
- = pawn   K = king
R = rook   Q = queen

Eighteen pieces, or children, are involved in this game, and another child is necessary to play the chess master who calls out the moves during the game.

Treat the chessboard as a grid. The eight horizontal squares on which the pieces stand may be lettered *A* through *H* (left to right). The vertical squares are numbered 1 through 8 (from the bottom of the board to the top of the board). White is set up at the bottom of the board.

Starting places:

Black King = D8   White Bishop = C8
Black Pawn = C7   White Pawn = F4
Black Bishop = A6   White Knight = H4
Black Knight = C6   White Pawn = E3
Black Bishop = D6   White Queen = C2
Black Knight = G6   White Rook = A1
Black Rook = A5   White King = C1
Black Queen = E5   White Rook = H1
Black Pawn = D4
Black Rook = C3

GAME:

White	Black
Kc1 — d1	Rc3 — d3
Qc2 x d3	Ng6 x h4
-e3 x d4	Bd6 - a3
Ra1 x a3	Nc6 x d4
Rh1 x h4	Qe5 x f4
Rh4 x f4	-c7 — c6
Kd1 — e1	Ba6 x c8
Ra3 x a5	-c6 — c5
Ra3 x c5	Bc8 — h3
Qd3 x d4 check	Kd7 — e7
Rf4 x f8 checkmate	

The Joust

The climax of any production is the joust between Lancelot and Gawain—or Mordred if you prefer a real villain. The audience should be divided and encouraged to cheer for one of the knights. Distribute crepe-paper flags with the colors of the knight they are applauding. The staging is simple: a long rope about 3 feet long divides the area. Shields and lances are necessary props, and squires hold swords for the battle on foot.

Sir Lancelot and Guinevere. [Whitney Barnett-Rhodes and Erin Bohmer.]

The horse props may cause the greatest difficulty, but are likely to be the hit of the show. Choose two well-adjusted children to be the horses' backsides. Each child must bend so that his or her head is touching the knight's back, and the child must hold on to the knight's waist. A "horse blanket" is thrown over the child. The two students—knight and horse—need to practice "trotting" together because the knight is also the front feet of the horse. The knight holds a lance in one hand and a stick pony head in the other. Once their movements are coordinated, they are ready to charge to the prerecorded sounds of hoofbeats. After a few misses, Lancelot is "thrown" from his horse, and Gawain dismounts to continue the fight. The children choreograph this ahead of time and predetermine a winner. If the students perform the joust for different audiences, alternate who the winner will be. If desired, each knight can have his "lady" tie her scarf to his sleeve—hence the expression, to wear one's heart on one's sleeve. The ladies can also start the cheering and rally the commoners. The audience will go wild.

Bibliography

Aliki. *A Medieval Feast*. New York: Thomas Y. Crowell, 1983.

Andronik, Catherine. *Quest for a King: Searching for the Real King Arthur*. New York: Atheneum, 1989.

Bortolussi, Lee Ann. *The Knights of the Round Table*. Milano, Italy: Dorset Press, 1991.

Byam, Michele. *Arms and Armor*. Eyewitness Books. New York, Alfred A. Knopf, 1988.

Caselli, Giovanni. *The Middle Ages.* History of Everyday Things. New York: Peter Bedrick, 1988.

Clare, John, ed. *Knights in Armor.* Living History. New York: Harcourt Brace Jovanovich, 1992.

Corbin, Carole Lynn. *Knights*. New York: Franklin Watts, 1989.

Corbishley, Mike. *The Medieval World*. Time Link Series. New York: Peter Bedrick, 1992.

Cosman, Madeleine Pelner. *Fabulous Feasts: Medieval Cookery and Ceremony*. 4th ed. New York: George Braziller, 1989.

Dickinson, Peter. *Merlin Dreams*. New York: Delacorte Press, 1988.

Doherty, Paul C. *King Arthur*. New York: Chelsea House, 1987.

Fradon, Dana. *Harold the Herald: A Book About Heraldry*. New York: Dutton Children's Books, 1990.

———. *The King's Fool: A Book About Medieval and Renaissance Fools*. New York: Dutton Children's Books, 1993.

———. *Sir Dana: A Knight as Told by His Trusty Armor*. New York: E. P. Dutton, 1988.

Grunfeld, Frederic, ed. *Games of the World*. New York: Holt, Rinehart & Winston, 1975.

Hastings, Selina. *Sir Gawain and the Green Knight*. New York: Lothrop, Lee & Shepard, 1981.

———. *Sir Gawain and the Loathly Lady*. New York: Lothrop, Lee & Shepard, 1985.

Heyer, Carol. *Excalibur*. Nashville, Tenn.: Ideals Children's Books, 1991.

Hodges, Margaret. *The Kitchen Knight: A Tale of King Arthur.* New York: Holiday House, 1990.

Hunt, Jonathan. *Illuminations.* New York: Bradbury Press, 1989.

Kidder, Harvey. *Illustrated Chess for Children.* Garden City, N.Y.: Doubleday, 1970.

Lanier, Sidney. *The Boy's King Arthur: Sir Thomas Malory's History of King Arthur and His Knights of the Round Table.* New York: Charles Scribner's Sons, 1989.

Lasker, Joe. *A Tournament of Kings.* New York: Harper Trophy, 1989.

Lister, Robin. *The Legend of King Arthur.* New York: Doubleday, 1988.

Macaulay, David. *Castle.* Boston: Houghton Mifflin, 1977.

MacDonald, Fiona. *The Middle Ages.* Facts on File. New York: Simon & Schuster, 1993.

MacDonald, Fiona, and Mark Bergin. *A Medieval Castle.* Inside Story Series. New York: Peter Bedrick, 1990.

Matthews, John, and Robert John Stewart. *Warriors of Arthur.* London: Blanford, 1987.

McCaughrean, Geraldine. *Saint George and the Dragon.* New York: Delacorte Press, 1989.

McLeod, William, and Ronald Mongredien. *Chess: For Young Beginners.* New York: Golden, 1975.

Morpurgo, Michael. *Arthur: High King of Britain.* New York: Harcourt Brace Jovanovich, 1994.

Osband, Gillian. *Castles.* New York: Orchard, 1991.

Perham, Molly. *King Arthur and the Legends of Camelot.* New York: Viking, 1993.

Platt, Richard. *Stephen Biesty's Cross Sections: Castles.* New York: Dorling Kindersley, 1994.

Pyle, Howard. *The Story of King Arthur and His Knights.* New York: Charles Scribner's Sons, 1984.

Sabuda, Robert. *Arthur and the Sword.* New York: Atheneum, 1995.

San Souci, Robert D. *Young Guinevere.* New York: Delacorte Press, 1993.

——. *Young Merlin.* New York: Doubleday, 1990.

Sancha, Sheila. *The Luttrell Village: Country Life in the Middle Ages.* New York: Thomas Y. Crowell, 1992.

Service, Pamela. *The Wizard of Wind and Rock.* New York: Atheneum, 1990.

Shannon, Mark. *Gawain and the Green Knight.* New York: G. P. Putnam's Sons, 1994.

Talbott, Hudson. *King Arthur and the Round Table.* New York: Morrow Junior Books, 1995.

——. *King Arthur: The Sword and the Stone.* New York: Morrow Junior Books, 1991.

Yolen, Jane. *Merlin and the Dragons.* New York: Dutton, 1994.

Software

Kid CAD. CD-ROM; Windows. Davidson Inc., Torrance, Calif.

2 Mount Olympus Revisited

Exploring Ancient Greece Through Olympian Myths

Table of Contents

The Personas of Mount Olympus	44
Step One: Prepersona Activities	50
Step Two: Decision Making	51
Step Three: Discovery Period	54
Culminating Activities	55
A. Dramas	57
B. Activities and Games	66
C. Displays	70
D. Spectacles	72
Bibliography	79

Mount Olympus Revisited

In the country of Greece there is a great mountain called Olympus. It stands so tall that its peak is hidden in the clouds. Once, long ago, it was believed that Mount Olympus was the home to a magnificent race of beings known as the Olympian gods. The thunderbolt-wielding Zeus and the ever-jealous queen of the gods, Hera, resided over Olympus. The enchantingly beautiful Aphrodite and the mysterious lord of the underworld, Hades, lived there also as well as the twins, Apollo and Artemis, who represented the many attributes of the sun and the moon. Many other gods and goddesses called Olympus home.

On the Earth below, terrible monsters such as the Cyclops and the Minotaur were defeated by such brave heroes as Odysseus and Theseus. There were so many mortals whose lives were touched by this superhuman race of gods and goddesses. The stories and adventures—known as the Greek myths—were so powerfully real to the ancient Greek civilization that they infiltrated every aspect of Greek life.

The following unit seeks to familiarize students with the Greek myths that still influence literature. Using the personas of Greek mythology, it is hoped that students will develop a personal connection to the ancient Greek civilization and enjoy experiencing life on Mount Olympus.

It would be unrealistic to attempt to do everything in this unit unless you devoted the entire school year to the subject. Choose what works for your class and your students' learning styles. One year you may concentrate on dramatizing the wealth of myths. Another year it might be more appealing to re-create the first Olympics. Any year is a good time to include "Athene's Persona Quilt." Whatever activities you choose to do, it will add to your student's understanding of Greek mythological characters and the culture that gave them life.

The Personas of Mount Olympus

The purpose of the persona list is to identify easily the main characters in Mount Olympus Revisited. It is in no way inclusive of all the characters found in Greek mythology but represents major personas as well as characters that are part of the dramas in this unit. The sketches are brief and should only act as a stimulus to students and teachers involved in the Olympus unit. More descriptive outlines of the personas will come from the children who choose them. This list is used in conjunction with the decision-making lesson after children become acquainted with several of the characters. Because these personas are the mainstay of Greek mythology, they can be found in many anthologies written for children, including Rockwell's *The Robber Baby: Stories from the Greek Myths;* Low's *The Macmillan Book of Greek Gods and Heroes;* McCaughrean's *Greek Myths;* and Oldfield's *Tales from Ancient Greece.*

The Olympian Gods

The Olympian gods were a mythical race of beings who physically and mentally resembled human beings. Their powers were great, and they looked like the Greeks but were more extreme. They were emotional and enjoyed toying with their human counterparts on Earth.

Aphrodite: Her parentage is uncertain, but she is probably a daughter of Zeus. She is the goddess of love and beauty though, ironically, she was the wife of the ugly Hephaestus.

Apollo: This strikingly handsome son of Zeus and Leto and twin of the goddess Artemis was the god of the sun, truth, healing, music, and poetry.

Ares: The violent son of Hera and Zeus, he was disliked by gods and mortals. He was the god of war. Interestingly, he and Aphrodite had a son, Eros—better known by his Roman name, Cupid.

Artemis: This twin sister of Apollo and daughter of Zeus and Leto was the goddess of the moon and the hunt. She chose not to marry, and her followers would not marry in her honor. She protected young animals and children.

Athene: The daughter of Zeus, she was born from his head wearing a suit of armor. She was the goddess of wisdom, and her symbol was the owl.

Demeter: Daughter of Rhea and Cronus, she is the goddess of the seasons.

Dionysus: This son of Zeus became the god of wine and vineyards. He often traveled in the company of satyrs, which were part human, part goat. He caused a great deal of trouble for King Midas when he gave him his golden wish.

Eris: Though a minor goddess, she played an important role in starting the Trojan War. She can be found in Low's *The Macmillan Book of Greek Gods and Heroes*, in the chapter on the Trojan War.

Eros: The son of Aphrodite and Ares, he is the only god never to grow up. The boy god was famous for shooting people with arrows that made them fall in love forever.

Hades: Son of Rhea and Cronus, he is the mysterious ruler of the underworld and god of the dead. His story is found in the tales of Persephone and Orpheus.

Hephaestus: The son of Hera and Zeus, he is the only ugly god. One day, Zeus became so angry with Hephaestus that he threw him off Mount Olympus. From that day forward, he had a limp. Hephaestus was the god of the forge and the Olympian blacksmith.

Hera: Daughter of Rhea and Cronus, she is Zeus's wife and queen of the gods. She was extremely jealous of her husband and spent much of her time punishing the women whom Zeus courted. She and Zeus had two children: Ares and Hephaestus. Hera was the goddess of marriage and was symbolized by the peacock.

Hermes: The son of Zeus and Maia, he was the messenger for the gods. He wore a winged helmet and winged sandals to deliver messages from Zeus. He protected travelers and thieves.

Hestia: Eldest daughter of Rhea and Cronus, she is the much-loved goddess of the hearth and home. Although she was goddess of the family, she never married. Fires that burned in the Greeks' homes were dedicated to Hestia.

Persephone: The daughter of Demeter, she was tricked into becoming the wife of Hades.

Poseidon: Son of Rhea and Cronus, he became the ruler of the sea. He used his trident—given to him by the Cyclops—to stir up the waters when he was angered. He was married to Amphitrite but often fell in love with sea nymphs and mortals. He gave man the gift of the horse.

Zeus: Son of the Titans, Rhea and Cronus, he is the king of the Olympian gods. Zeus established Mount Olympus as his home and took his sister, Hera, as his wife. Zeus is the lord of the skies and ruled with his lightning bolts. Many of his adventures involve his courtships with other goddesses, nymphs, and human women.

The Titans

The Titans were a race of giants and the children of Gaea and Uranus. When the Olympians came into power, some of the Titans—including Cronus and Atlas—were punished. Others chose to fight on the side of the Olympians.

Atlas: The brother of Cronus, he fought against the Olympians in the great war. He was condemned to carry the world on his shoulders.

Cronus: After hearing a prophesy that one of his children would overthrow him, Cronus devoured each of them at birth. Rhea tricked him with the sixth child and fed Cronus a stone instead.

Epimetheus: He was commissioned by Zeus to fill the world with marvelous creations. The Titan created all the animals and birds of the world. His wife was the beautiful but curious Pandora. He is found in stories about Prometheus and Pandora.

Prometheus: The father of mankind who molded mortals from clay in the image of the Olympian gods. He loved his creations so much that he gave them a special gift: fire.

Rhea: The Titan mother of all the Olympian gods, five of her children were fed to their father, Cronus, against her wishes. She saved her sixth child, Zeus, from this fate by feeding Cronus a stone wrapped in a blanket.

The Heroes

The following list does not include many of the great heroes, including Hector, Ajax, and Bellerophon and his winged horse, Pegasus. Feel free to add them to the myths you choose to retell.

Achilles: One of the great Greek heroes of the Trojan War and the subject of Homer's epic poem *The Iliad*. His mother wanted to protect him from all injuries when he was still a baby, so she held him by the ankle and dipped him into the River Styx. During the war, he was fatally wounded when an arrow pierced his ankle—the hero's vulnerable point, which is known today as an Achilles' heel.

Heracles: Better known by his Roman name, Hercules, he was the remarkably strong son of Zeus. He was despised by the goddess Hera, and she caused him finally to go into a terrible rage during which he killed his family. His punishment: to complete 12 impossible labors.

Jason: The rightful heir to the throne of Iolcus, his uncle made him prove his worth by bringing him the famed Golden Fleece. Jason's story is found in Fisher's *Jason and the Golden Fleece*.

Odysseus: One of the great Greek heroes of the Trojan War. It took him 10 years to sail home to Ithaca and his faithful wife, Penelope. His adventures are related in Fisher's *Cyclops*.

Oedipus: Not truly a hero, this son of King Laius of Thebes grew up to unknowingly fulfill a horrible prophecy: He killed his own father and unknowingly took his mother for his queen. His greatest adventure was answering the riddle of the Sphinx.

Perseus: The son of Zeus and the grandson of the king of Argos. Perseus beheaded the Gorgon Medusa. His story can be found in Hutton's *Perseus*.

Theseus: The son of King Aegeus or possibly the god Poseidon. Theseus volunteered to be one of the sacrificial youths sent to Crete to be fed to the Minotaur. His story is told in Hutton's *Theseus and the Minotaur*.

The Monsters

Some of the world's most imaginative and frightening monsters can be found in the myths. Many colorful ones, such as the Chimera and the Hydra, do not appear here but would make wonderful additions.

Charon: Not truly a monster, he was, however, a mysterious character from the underworld. He is the ferryman who takes the dead across the River Styx.

Medusa: One of the three Gorgons, Medusa was so hideous that a person would turn to stone after just gazing at her. Her story is found in Hutton's *Perseus*.

Minotaur: The stepson of King Minos of Crete and the half brother of Ariadne, Minotaur had the body of a man but the head of a bull. His story is told in Hutton's *Theseus and the Minotaur*.

Polyphemus the Cyclops: Son of Poseidon, Polyphemus was the one-eyed giant who held Odysseus's men captive in his cave and ate them one by one. Fisher's book, *Cyclops*, tells how Odysseus dealt with the cyclops.

Sphinx: This monster had the body of a lion and the head of a woman. She watched over a road near Thebes and killed anyone who could not answer the riddle, "What walks on four legs in the morning, two in the afternoon, and three in the evening?" (a human).

The Mortals

One definition for a mortal might be an ordinary person who lives and dies. The following list contains no such beings. The moment a mortal has an encounter with a god, an extraordinary event has occurred. There are many personas—Menelaus, Agamemnon, Clytemnestra, and countless others—who could be added to this group. Your persona selections will vary depending on the myths you choose to read to your class. This list stretches the term *mortal* by including nymphs as well.

Andromeda: The unfortunate daughter of Cepheus and Cassiopeia who was to be sacrificed to the sea monster to save the Ethiopian people.

Arachne: An unfortunate mortal who had the nerve to challenge the goddess Athene's weaving skills. This act of hubris, or pride, doomed her to a life of eternal spinning as the world's first spider.

Ariadne: The daughter of King Minos and the half sister to the monster Minotaur. She fell in love with the hero Theseus and helped him travel through the labyrinth to kill the beast. Her story is told in Orgel's *Ariadne, Awake!*

Atalanta: When Atalanta's father insisted she marry, Atalanta set up a contest in which she would marry the man who could outrun her. All others would be put to death. Her story is found in Martin's *The Race of the Golden Apples*.

Cassiopeia: The proud queen of Ethiopia, she bragged that her daughter, Andromeda, was more beautiful than the sea nymphs.

Cepheus: The king of Ethiopia and the husband of Cassiopeia. When his wife insulted Poseidon and the sea nymphs, he was forced to sacrifice his daughter, Andromeda, to the ferocious monster. In the end, Cepheus and the sea monster were also turned into constellations.

Daedulus: The great architect and inventor from Athens was imprisoned with his young son, Icarus. He designed wings from bird feathers and wax so that he might escape, but tragedy resulted. His story is told in Yolen's *Wings*.

Echo: A lovely wood nymph who was condemned to repeat the last words others uttered because she had annoyed the goddess Hera.

Helen: The most beautiful woman on Earth and the wife of King Menelaus of Sparta. Aphrodite offered her as a prize to Paris of Troy if he chose Aphrodite as the winner of the beauty contest. He did, and Helen was given to Paris, thus beginning the Trojan War.

Hippomenes: The young man who, with the help of the goddess Aphrodite, won the lovely Atalanta for his bride by winning a race. His story is found in Martin's *The Race of the Golden Apples*.

Icarus: The son of the great master builder, Daedulus. He was imprisoned in a tower with his father, who then created wings with which he and Icarus would escape the tower. Icarus was warned not to fly too close to the sun, but he did not listen to his father. Yolen's *Wings* is one book that tells Icarus' story.

Midas: A wealthy but greedy king, he was a favorite plaything of the gods. Dionysus granted him his famous wish: to have the golden touch. His story is retold in Oldfield's *Tales from Ancient Greece*.

Narcissus: An extremely handsome youth who caught his reflection in a pool of water and immediately fell in love with himself.

Pandora: The first woman on Earth and the wife of the Titan Epimetheus, Pandora was ideal in every way except her extreme curiosity. She was told not to open a box that the gods gave her as a wedding gift, but she could not resist.

Paris: The son of King Priam of Troy who was asked to judge a beauty contest among Hera, Athene, and Aphrodite. When he chose Aphrodite, Aphrodite gave him Helen as a prize, and that started the Trojan War.

Step One: Prepersona Activities

1. Read several myths to children to introduce some of the characters of Greek mythology. Those who are unfamiliar with the long names may have some difficulties grasping the stories, but explain to students that they will get to know these characters more at a later period and that they should keep in mind the names of some of the characters they wish to learn more about.

    Some great introductory books are Yolen's *Wings*; Hutton's *Perseus* and *Theseus and the Minotaur*; Fisher's *The Olympians: Great Gods and Goddesses of Ancient Greece*, *Jason and the Golden Fleece*, and *Cyclops*; Hodges's *The Arrow and the Lamp: The Story of Psyche*; and Martin's *The Race of the Golden Apples*. Some wonderful anthologies include Rockwell's *The Robber Baby: Stories from the Greek Myths*; Low's *The Macmillan Book of Greek Gods and Heroes*; McCaughrean's *Greek Myths*; and Oldfield's *Tales from Ancient Greece*.

2. Start to introduce the curriculum-content areas of ancient Greece. These will be explored as personas, but begin to introduce some of the concepts. Some topics that might be covered are Greek city-states, Athens, Sparta, Greek medicine and science, and democracy.

3. Develop a strategy to introduce children to role playing: Read the story of Prometheus. There are many variations of this story. One excellent version is from McCaughrean's anthology, *Greek Myths*. Have the children reenact the story by role-playing the characters of Zeus, Prometheus, Epimetheus, Athene, and the clay humans.

To encourage students to start thinking in the first person, ask them the following questions. Their response can be written or oral.

A. What if you were Zeus? Why would you not want these clay humans to have fire? How do you feel about what Prometheus did?

B. What if you were the clay humans that Prometheus created? What would you do with the fire? (Remember, at this time in history there was no electricity.)

C. What if you were Epimetheus? How would you feel about what your brother did? What kinds of "gifts" would you give to the animals you created?

D. What if you were Prometheus? Why do you want to give your clay humans the gift of fire? Knowing your punishment, if you had the chance to do it again, would you?

E. What if you were Athene? Why would you help Prometheus?

Step Two: Decision Making

Below is a review of the decision-making process. Once students have heard some of the myths, the persona element can be introduced.

1. Explain to students that they will be choosing a persona and doing projects as that persona. Though some of the children may have difficulties with some of the more lengthy names, explain to them that they will become more familiar with the names and stories. Talk about some of the culminating projects. Explain that there are many different types of projects and that each child will be taking part in several projects. Warn them as well that some of the well-known characters, such as Zeus, will probably be in many of the performances. These characters will require much more work and research. Students should be encouraged to start thinking about the characters they will feel most comfortable researching and about the types of culminating projects in which they will wish to participate.

2. Each student will be asked to make three character choices and to give reasons why they want to be each character. These reasons are important if two or more children want to be the same persona.

3. Place a copy of the Mount Olympus criteria for decision making in a visible place. Encourage students to invent additional criteria. See the work sheet in this chapter for a copy of the criteria.

4. Review some of the personas. Emphasize some of the lesser-known characters, and have a list of the personas for student reference when they are making their choices.

5. Have students complete the Mount Olympus decision-making work sheet.

6. As part of the lesson that follows, talk with each student individually. Students should be happy with their persona.

Name _____

MOUNT OLYMPUS DECISION-MAKING WORK SHEET

DECISION: WHICH PERSONA DO I WANT TO BECOME FOR MOUNT OLYMPUS?

Below is a list of some of your choices:

    GODS: Aphrodite, Apollo, Ares, Artemis, Athene, Demeter, Dionysus, Eris, Eros, Hades, Hephaestus, Hera, Hermes, Hestia, Persephone, Poseidon, Zeus

    TITANS: Atlas, Cronus, Epimetheus, Prometheus, Rhea

    MORTALS: Andromeda, Arachne, Ariadne, Atalanta, Cassiopeia, Cepheus, Daedulus, Echo, Helen, Hippomenes, Icarus, Midas, Narcissus, Pandora, Paris

    HEROES: Achilles, Heracles, Jason, Odysseus, Oedipus, Perseus, Theseus

    MONSTERS: Charon, Cyclops, Medusa, Minotaur, Sphinx

Answer the questions on the following page. Use your answers to help you make a decision. Give several reasons for your decision.

Give three choices in order of preference.

1. _____

2. _____

3. _____

Name _____

MOUNT OLYMPUS DECISION-MAKING WORK SHEET
Page 2

DECISION: WHICH PERSONA DO I WANT TO BECOME FOR MOUNT OLYMPUS?

1. Why do I want to be this persona?

2. What do I like about the persona of the character?

3. Do I want to have a big part in the performance?

4. Will I do extra research concerning this character?

5. Will I be able to design and make the costume?

Step Three: Discovery Period

Although students should be encouraged to collect information about their persona, the primary purpose of this unit is to explore the historical period. Within this unit, the teacher can introduce various aspects of ancient Greece, and students can use library time as research time to explore the period through their personas. Students may use the following questions to gain insight into the period:

1. Compare Sparta and Athens. In which city would your persona most likely want to live? Why? (Note: Instead of a written report the first part can be done using a Venn diagram.)

2. Many inventions, discoveries, and great ideas came from ancient Greece. Describe one, and explain its importance. If your persona met this Greek inventor, discoverer, or philosopher, what would he or she think? Some interesting combinations are:

   A. Athene, goddess of wisdom, and Socrates,* famous philosopher and teacher, can discuss what qualities make a good student and teacher.

   B. Apollo, god of poetry, and Odysseus, the subject of the great epic *The Odyssey*, along with famous poet Homer.*

   C. Achilles, Trojan War hero, or Ares, god of war, can discuss military strategies with Alexander the Great.*

   D. Plato,* writer of *The Republic*, discusses democracy with King Midas and King Cepheus.

   E. Prometheus, creator of mankind, can talk with Hippocrates,* founder of medicine. Atlas can report on Greek medicine, especially how to cure a backache.

   F. Pythagoras,* mathematician and philosopher, can talk to Daedulus, creator of the labyrinth, about the importance of math in their daily lives.

3. What role did your persona play in ancient Greek society? Describe your importance to the Greeks?

In addition, students may report on various topics. Following is a list of topics that certain types of personas may want to pursue:

Major Gods: Aphrodite, Apollo, Athene, Demeter, Hades, Hera, Persephone, Poseidon, Zeus

    Democracy   The territory of ancient Greece

    City-states

Minor Gods: Ares, Artemis, Dionysus, Eris, Eros, Hephaestus, Hermes, Hestia

    Poetry   The arts

    Theater   Architecture

*This is an historical personality not included in our persona list.

Titans: Atlas, Cronus, Epimetheus, Prometheus, Rhea
  Science
  Medicine

Mortals: Echo, Narcissus, Paris, etc.
  Everyday life in ancient Greece
  Farming, fishing, food, and family

Heroes: Heracles, Odysseus, etc. and Monsters: Medusa, Polyphemus the Cyclops, etc.
  Trojan War   The first Olympics
  Importance of physical strength and athletics in Greek society

Students could work in groups or separately. Each group could report to the class about a chosen topic.

Who Am I? Work Sheet

Students can create a page of their own using the "Who Am I" work sheet page 56. The questionnaire helps ease students into the writing process and encourages them to think in the first person. Students will also design a picture of their personas to accompany the creative writing.

Culminating Activities

For an exciting culminating activity, have students perform a Greek drama or re-create the first Olympics. The Greek dramas are the stories of the personas. The first Olympics are composed of performances and games that use mythology as a stepping-stone into the world of ancient Greece.

Below are the types of culminating events that are used for this unit. Select a limited number of activities.

Dramas. Theater was an important part of the lives of the ancient Greeks. Use the skits in the book, or have your students create their own. The performances in the book re-create many of the stories of the personas so that students can expand and enhance each skit.

Activities and Games. If you wish, set aside a day called Greek Olympics Day. Physical education may be integrated into this part, and children can compete in their own Olympic games. Or invite parents and possibly other classes to see "Mount Olympus Alive."

Displays. Displays help bring the world of ancient Greece to your classroom or library. Displays might include colorful bowls and printed togas.

Spectacles. Spectacles differ from traditional drama inasmuch as they can include a large number of children. Whether it is a dance or the first Olympics, a spectacle is always a crowd pleaser.

Student's Name _____

Persona's Name _____

MOUNT OLYMPUS WHO AM I? WORK SHEET

Now that you have returned to the golden age of Greece, you must let everyone know who you are. In no fewer than five sentences, tell me who you are.

Examples of what you might include:

1. Describe what sort of person you are: god, hero, monster, mortal, Titan, etc.

2. Do you have special talents or powers?

3. Are you related to anyone on Mount Olympus?

4. Tell me about an interesting adventure your persona had.

5. Do you know how your life will end?

6. How would you describe yourself: brave, shy, mysterious, obnoxious, arrogant, clever, romantic, beautiful, loyal, dedicated, feisty, fiendish, fair, ferocious, humble, cold-blooded, evil, honest, powerful, charismatic, smart, curious?

From *The Persona Book*. © 1997. Katherine Lallier and Nancy Marino. TIP. (800) 237-6124.

A. Dramas

The following is a collection of performance scripts based on Greek mythology. Students can expand these dramas or create their own. Limit stage instructions, and encourage students to role-play. The poems may be used as is or serve as a model for students who wish to create poetry about other characters.

Instead of a narrator, these skits use the traditional Greek chorus. In ancient Greek plays, the chorus was used to move the plot along.

Pandora

Characters:
Aphrodite
Ares
Athene
Epimetheus
Hephaestus
Pandora
Prometheus
Zeus
Two voices in box (unseen by audience)

HEPHAESTUS: I am Hephaestus, the god of the forge. I'm kind of ugly, and you'll notice I limp. But all the gods on Mount Olympus like me well enough. Something interesting happened to me when the world began. I don't think it was nice, but Zeus is in charge, and I try to do what he says. In the very beginning, the gods ruled over an empty world. So Zeus had a job for the Titan brothers.

ZEUS: Prometheus, Epimetheus, I was wondering if you could do me a favor. Earth is—well, how should I say it? Well, it's kind of boring. I think the two of you should make some living creatures to make things more exciting.

EPIMETHEUS: That sounds great! I already have some great ideas. What would you think of a creature that carries its house on its back? Or how about one with a neck as long as its whole body? This is gonna be fun!

ZEUS: Whatever you two plan I'm sure I'll like it. Get back to me as soon as you are done. (*Exit Zeus*)

EPIMETHEUS: We'll get started this afternoon. (*Prometheus sits and watches as Epimetheus makes animal after animal.*)

From *The Persona Book.* © 1997. Katherine Lallier and Nancy Marino. TIP. (800) 237-6124.

EPIMETHEUS: Hey, Prometheus. Check this one out: animals with feathers. I'm going to give them the gift of flight. And look at this: a beaver with a flat tail so that he can pat down mud and build dams. Get a load of this. I call it whale. It swims in the ocean, but it breathes the air. There is no end to my bright ideas. Hey, what are you making? You've been sitting over that lump of clay forever.

(*Prometheus takes soil and water and molds a human.*)

PROMETHEUS: I think I'll call it a human. He's going to be a miniversion of us. I'm going to make him look like Zeus, but he won't have a thunderbolt. He's kind of cute. What do you think?

EPIMETHEUS: Looks good. What gift are you going to give him?

PROMETHEUS: It has to be a wonderful gift. Maybe claws?

(*Epimetheus looks into a box marked Gifts.*)

EPIMETHEUS: Claws are all gone.

PROMETHEUS: I know. Wings!

EPIMETHEUS: No can do. Birds got it.

PROMETHEUS: Courage?

EPIMETHEUS: Nada.

PROMETHEUS: Gee. All the good stuff's gone. Wait a minute. I have an idea!

(*Enter Hephaestus*)

HEPHAESTUS: This is where I fit in. Prometheus sneaked up onto Olympus and asked me for some fire.

PROMETHEUS: Come on, Hephaestus. Just a tiny spark?

HEPHAESTUS: Are you kidding? Zeus will have a fit.

PROMETHEUS: Then I'll just take some. (*He runs away with a torch.*)

HEPHAESTUS: That is just what he did. Now I didn't tell Zeus, but he found out just the same.

(*Enter Zeus with Ares*)

ZEUS:	Prometheus! You little wart! Where on Mount Olympus are you? How in Zeus' name did those little art projects of yours get fire? I don't recall giving you permission to touch my things. Next, you'll be giving thunderbolts to the birds! This time you've really annoyed me, Prometheus. Ares, take this little Titan away. *(Exit Zeus)*
ARES:	With pleasure, Zeus. *(To Prometheus)* Wait till you see what I have got planned for you. First I'm going to tie you to this cliff. Everyday for the rest of your life—which is forever—eagles are going to come and peck out your liver. Bet that'll hurt! I just love being the god of destruction and war! *(Exit Ares)*
HEPHAESTUS:	Zeus was just as mad at the humans as he was at Prometheus, however. You'd never know it though. Part of his plan was to have me forge the first woman.

(Enter Aphrodite with Pandora and Ares. Exit Hephaestus.)

APHRODITE:	I'll take it from here, Hephaestus. Zeus put me in charge of this woman. Her name is Pandora. As you can see, she is beautiful. That's because I'm the goddess of love and beauty, and I made her that way. All of the gods and goddesses gave her something special. She's a gift, a present for Epimetheus. Ares is going to deliver the package.
ARES:	Epimetheus, come out, come out wherever you are. Do not worry. Zeus isn't mad at you. Just because your brother messed up big time doesn't mean he's going to take out his anger on you. Actually, it's just the opposite. He has a little present for you: a wife. She even comes with a little token of the gods' esteem in that box there. *(Pandora, holding a box, is given to Epimetheus.)* One thing: Don't open the box. Zeus said it wouldn't be a good idea. Good luck. *(Exit Ares)*
APHRODITE:	Let's take a look at the happy couple.
PANDORA:	I hope you enjoyed supper.
EPIMETHEUS:	It was delicious.
PANDORA:	When do you suppose we can open that box from Zeus? Ares said it was filled with little tokens from the gods.

EPIMETHEUS:	It's not up to me. Zeus will let us know when we can open it.
PANDORA:	How about one little peek?
EPIMETHEUS:	Pandora, I'll give you anything you want, but you cannot have that!
PANDORA:	You're no fun.
EPIMETHEUS:	Neither is the wrath of Zeus. One day I should introduce you to my brother. He could tell you a thing or two about not listening to the gods. *(Exits)*
PANDORA:	Okay, okay. I won't touch it. *(She starts cleaning near the chest.)* It's probably just full of something boring. On the other hand, it's probably filled with really neat stuff. After all, this is no ordinary present. This isn't from any ordinary person. It's from the gods—the gods of Mount Olympus. What could it hurt to shake it a little?

From *The Persona Book.* © 1997. Katherine Lallier and Nancy Marino. TIP. (800) 237-6124.

BOX:	Hey, who's shaking the box?
PANDORA:	Oh, it's only me, Pandora. Who is in there?
BOX:	Why don't you open the box and find out?
PANDORA:	I was told not to touch the box.
BOX:	You obviously didn't listen to that rule, or we wouldn't be awake from all that shaking. Come on, open up.
PANDORA:	I may be curious, but I'm not stupid. Tell me your name first.
BOX:	My name is Deception. In here with me are some close friends named Hate, Pain, Sickness, and Injustice. Pleased to meet you.

(Pandora freezes and Aphrodite enters.)

APHRODITE:	Sorry to stop the action, but there is something you need to know. The Earth was paradise back then. Pandora didn't have the slightest idea what hunger and hatred and poverty and cruelty were. Let's see what Pandora does.
PANDORA:	Well, since you told me your names, I guess it could not hurt to open the lid. *(Pandora opens the box.)*
BOX:	You idiot! You let us out! We're free! We're free! We can wreak havoc on the world thanks to Pandora!
PANDORA:	Oh no, what have I done?
VOICE IN BOX:	Don't worry, Pandora. I am Hope. I will try to help people cope with all the evils. At least when I am around, the world will be able to bear all the unhappiness you have turned loose!
HEPHAESTUS:	Well, that's how the world inherited evil. But that's how it got hope too. And hopefully, hope is stronger than any sadness that humans have to face.

Judgment of Paris

Characters:
Aphrodite
Athene
Eris
Eros
Helen
Hera
Paris
Zeus
Chorus

CHORUS: The terrible war between the Greeks and the Trojans began because of an argument between three goddesses. It all started because of a nasty little goddess named Eris.

ERIS: They never invite me anywhere. How come all the other goddesses were invited to the wedding feast? Don't they like me? Well, I'll show them. I'm going to play a little trick on the whole bunch of them. I'll take this golden apple and leave a little message on it: For the Most Beautiful.

(Eris tosses the apple into the banquet.)

ATHENE: Who is this for? It says "For the Most Beautiful." Well, it must be for me.

HERA: Let me see that, Athene. It says, "For the Most Beautiful." Don't you realize that that's me. After all, I am the queen of Olympus.

APHRODITE: Excuse me, girls, but that was obviously meant for me, goddess of love and beauty. Remember?

ATHENE: It's mine, Aphrodite.

HERA: Give it back, Athene.

APHRODITE: Hera, I said it's mine!

ZEUS: Ladies, what's all this arguing about?

APHRODITE: We discovered this golden apple, and Hera and Athene don't seem to understand that it was meant for me.

ATHENE: Father, it is Aphrodite who doesn't understand!

HERA: Husband, it belongs to me! Tell them.

From *The Persona Book*. © 1997. Katherine Lallier and Nancy Marino. TIP. (800) 237-6124.

A. Dramas: Judgment of Paris

ZEUS: I don't think I'm going to touch this with a 10-foot thunderbolt. Go to Mount Ida and ask the shepherd prince, Paris, to judge your beauty contest.

ATHENE, HERA, APHRODITE: Fine!

CHORUS: The three goddesses flew to Mount Ida in search of Paris. Each goddess had a private moment with him.

HERA: Paris, as you know, I am queen of the gods, but don't let that influence you—too much. If you give the apple to me, I shall give you great power and riches.

PARIS: Thank you, Queen Hera. That is very generous of you.

ATHENE: How are you today, Paris?

PARIS: Very well, Athene, and you?

ATHENE: I would be much happier if the apple were mine. How would you like to be the most glorious warrior that ever was? I could arrange it, you know.

PARIS: I'll remember your offer, good Athene.

APHRODITE: Paris, dear, I am so glad you're judging the contest. You can tell a beautiful girl when you see one. If you choose me, I shall give you the best gift of all: The most beautiful woman in the world will be yours. Think about it, Paris.

PARIS: Thank-you, beautiful Aphrodite. I'll be making my decision soon. Boy, how lucky can a guy get? One minute I'm counting sheep, and the next I'm judging a beauty contest between three of the most powerful goddesses on Mount Olympus. They offered me some really great bribes—I mean gifts—too.

Gee, what do I want? To be a famous warrior or to be rich and powerful? Maybe the most beautiful woman in the world would be a good prize. Okay, I've made my decision. You can all come back. I hereby award the golden apple to . . . Aphrodite.

APHRODITE: Told you, girls!

From *The Persona Book*. © 1997. Katherine Lallier and Nancy Marino. TIP. (800) 237-6124.

HERA:	What!
ATHENE:	You'll regret this, Paris! *(Exits with Hera)*
PARIS:	Oh, goddess of love, who is the most beautiful woman in the world?
APHRODITE:	Why, Helen of Greece, of course. Hundreds of suitors tried to win her, and now she is the wife of the king of Sparta. But I shall make her fall in love with you.
PARIS:	This is great.
APHRODITE:	Eros, my son, find Helen and shoot her with your magical arrow.
EROS:	I will go this minute, Mother.

(Eros finds Helen and brings her to Paris.)

EROS:	Helen, this is Paris. Do you like him?
HELEN:	He's so cute. I would be happy to leave Sparta and stay here in Troy with you, Paris.
PARIS:	This is great. And people thought I was crazy to judge that beauty contest.
CHORUS:	Helen's husband was not about to let Paris take Helen for a prize. So war broke out between the Greeks and the Trojans, and to this day, the long and terrible battle has been known as the Trojan War.

Heroes

Characters:
- Achilles
- Heracles
- Jason
- Odysseus
- Perseus
- Theseus

All: We are the heroes of Ancient Greece
The greatest of mortals, no doubt
The warriors and keepers of the peace
The ones the tales are told about

Perseus: I am Perseus with the magic shield
It is the monster Medusa I seek
If I look at her face, my fate is sealed
I'll turn to stone if I take a peek

Jason: I am searching for the famed Golden Fleece
For I am Jason of the ship Argo
If I don't find it, there'll be no peace
If it's not part of the Argonaut's cargo

Theseus: I'm Theseus, hero of the labyrinth
It's my job to kill a beast
It's a horrible monster, the Minotaur
And he's been eating Athens' young for a feast

Achilles: I am the great warrior, Achilles
I fought in the Trojan War
Some people thought I had weak knees
But it was my heels that were really sore

Heracles: I'm Heracles of the 12 labors
It was punishment for a terrible crime
I tackled a lion, a Hydra, and a bull
In all, it took 12 years of my time

Odysseus: I am the hero of *The Odyssey*
Odysseus is my given name
I outwitted the Cyclopes to be free
It's one of the adventures that gave me fame

All: We are the heroes of ancient Greece
The greatest of mortals, no doubt
The warriors and keepers of the peace
The ones the tales are told about

From *The Persona Book*. © 1997. Katherine Lallier and Nancy Marino. TIP. (800) 237-6124.

Oedipus

Oedipus: Hi, I'm Oedipus. Please don't call me Eddie. I need your help. You see that? It's called the Sphinx. Part lion, part woman, all mean. If I don't figure out the answer to her riddle, I'm a deadipus Oedipus. Hopefully one of you will know the answer and save me from an awful fate. Here goes: What walks on four feet in the morning, two feet in the afternoon, and three feet in the evening? Anyone?

If someone guesses correctly, congratulate him or her.

If not, the answer is: Man. Man crawls on all fours at the beginning of his life, stands tall on two feet in the middle of his life, and uses a cane near the end of his life.

B. Activities and Games

Pandora's Box

A large, gift-wrapped box can be used as Pandora's box. Create a station for your library or classroom. Encourage students to stump their classmates with a question about their persona or ancient Greece. Students develop questions using a group of about five books that are chosen by the teacher or librarian. The books are kept near Pandora's box for reference. Using these books, students create a question and the answer and list the source of the answer.

Before passing out the form in this chapter, number each one and then have students fill them out. Give the form to a student who is acting as the game director. The game director checks the answer and makes sure the question is valid. The student then tears the form at the dotted line and places the top section in Pandora's box. The game director keeps the bottom part as the answer key.

When students are finished with their projects, they may go to Pandora's box and answer a question. They may use the five books near the game as a resource and as a way to improve their information-seeking skills. When they get an answer, they can go to the student who is the game director. The game director checks their answer. Correct answers are rewarded with a bookmark or sticker. Below is a sample question.

Question: I, Heracles, had to go on 12 dangerous tasks. What was my second?

Answer: Killing the Hydra

Source: *Greek Myths*, by Geraldine McCaughrean

Student's Name _____

Persona's Name _____

PANDORA'S BOX

QUESTION NUMBER _____

QUESTION: _____

_____

_____

_____

_____

_____

_____

- -

Student's Name _____

PANDORA'S BOX ANSWER KEY

QUESTION NUMBER _____

ANSWER: _____

_____

_____

_____

_____

_____

SOURCE: _____

From *The Persona Book*. © 1997. Katherine Lallier and Nancy Marino. TIP. (800) 237-6124.

The 12 Labors of Heracles

This event can be designed to be a competition between students or a noncompetitive participation event. The object of the course is to complete the 12 labors. Award one point for each successfully completed labor. This can be an event in the Olympics. If you wish, you may award medals. For 10 to 12 points, award a gold medal. For 8 to 9, award a silver; for 7 and under, a bronze. In a spacious area, set up 12 stations that represent the 12 labors of Heracles. Have students create signs for each station.

Number	Herculean Task	Student Task
1.	Kill the Nemean Lion	Throw a hoola-hoop over a stuffed toy lion.
2.	Kill the Hydra (9 snake heads)	9 jumps of a jump rope.
3.	Bring back the white stag	Fish for a white disk of paper. In a box, place circles of colored construction paper. Make sure to include many white pieces. Place a paper clip on each paper. Tie a magnet to a string. Allow child to fish for the white paper using the string.
4.	Capture boar	Bowl down 3 bowling pins. If you wish, you may place a picture of a pig on the pins.
5.	Clean the stable of Augeas	Push a ball with a broom from one point to another.
6.	Get rid of the Stymphalian birds	With a badminton racket, hit the birdie straight up in the air 3 times.
7.	Catch the Cretan bull	Create a ring toss using two wrapping-paper tubes or two soda bottles for the bull's horns.
8.	Get the man-eating mares	Students must hop on one foot for 10 seconds holding a stick pony.
9.	Capture the Amazon girdle	Hoola-hoop for 5 seconds.
10.	Capture cattle guarded by a monster and a two-headed dog	Limbo.
11.	Bring the golden apples	Choose box that has apple under it.
12.	Capture Cerberus in the Underworld	Charon's coin toss. Toss a coin, and have student call heads or tails.

Persona Poems

The poems of ancient Greece are a major contribution to Western literature. *The Odyssey* and *The Iliad* were epic poems that told stories about adventures. Have children create poems about their personas. Two of the poems below are limericks. Feel free to use any poetry style with which you and your students are familiar.

Icarus

There once was a boy who could fly
His father said not to go high
With wings made of wax
These are the sad facts
When they melted, he fell from the sky

Midas

King Midas was king. Don't you see
He was also as rich as could be
But his touch was real cold
Everything turned to gold
Boy I hope that he doesn't touch me

Arachne

My name is Arachne
And the awful fact be
What a goddess did to me.
Have you heard of Athene?
There is no one meaner
The reason you soon will see.

I was a weaver, a spinner of thread
A talent if ever there was one.
I told all the nymphs I was best in the land
Or anyone under the sun.

If you don't know it, I'll tell you right now
Athene's the goddess of weaving.
She heard of my boasts, and I didn't deny it
I'm not the kind for deceiving.

There was a contest to see who was best
And I'm no ordinary kid.
Athene was worried, my weaving was good
So she turned me from Arachne to Arachnid.

According to the Greeks, I'm the very first spider
And it was all because of my pride.
I learned a lesson about bragging that day
To Athene, I should have lied.

Modern-Day Mythology

Recess in Greece is a software program by Morgan Interactive. It retraces the steps of Homer's *Iliad* and tests students' knowledge of ancient Greece. The character who takes students on their tour is Hermes the messenger. Hermes is dressed as a biker complete with a Harley Davidson. Have your students think of how their personas would act, dress, and behave in modern times.

The First Library

Ancient Greece was famous for its libraries. Librarians collected and organized information. In a corner of your classroom or library, place a box of about 20 to 30 nonfiction books, videos, and pictures on five or six different subjects. (Don't forget to block out the Dewey classification numbers.) Make copies of the work sheet, and place them near the box. This could be used as a workstation, and it introduces students to the concept of subject classification.

C. Displays

Athene's Persona Quilt

In honor of Athene, the talented weaver, the personas are woven together in a colorful quilt. Each student's "Who Am I?" work sheet and accompanying drawing is a "patch." After individual patches have been created, use a large blanket or piece of mural paper as a background. Arrange patches on the quilt.

Personas on Computer

Have Mount Olympus meet high technology by creating a display with your computer. Use a digital video camera, such as QuickCam, to take pictures of your students dressed as their personas. This camera allows still and motion images to be captured for your computer.

Greek Bowls

Anthropologists have learned much about the culture of ancient Greece by studying scenes painted on Greek pottery. Everyday life and mythological scenes were painted on dishes, vases, and plates. Students can make their own pottery by using papier-mâché.

Make a paste out of flour and water. Have students take newspapers strips, dip them in the flour-and-water mixture, and place them on the outside of a bowl. (The bowl acts as a mold and allows the students to make the form.) Continue placing strips on the bowl, making several layers, until the entire bowl is covered. After the papier-mâché dries, trim the rim and remove the papier-mâché from the bowl. Have students study the types of scenes and patterns on ancient Greek pottery so that they can paint their dried bowls.

Name _____

Ancient Greece Library Work Sheet

Congratulations.

You have been named the chief librarian of the great Library of Athens. This is a big responsibility. The chief librarian must ensure that all the information can be found when it is needed.

Your first mission is to look through the materials in the box and to decide how it should be arranged. Should the books be sorted by size, subject, author's name, or color?

Arrange your materials in the order you have decided. Remember that you want to make it easy for your library users to find the information they need. Use the space below to explain how you arranged your materials and why you chose your method.

_____

_____

_____

_____

_____

_____

_____

_____

_____

Printed Togas

After students research patterns from ancient Greece, they can make a print for their togas. Students should choose a pattern from the pottery or artwork of ancient Greece and re-create the pattern by cutting a sponge in the same shape as the pattern. It should be a small pattern, one they would like to repeat. Dip one side of the sponge into tempera paints. Place it carefully on a piece of cloth, and repeat the pattern around the hem. An old T-shirt may be used, or a pillowcase makes a great toga. Cut a hole in the top and at the arms, and tie at the waist. With the authentic Greek pattern on the bottom, your gods and goddesses will look as if they just stepped off of Mount Olympus.

D. Spectacles

Syrtos, A Greek Folk Dance

Dancing was held in high regard in ancient Greece. The first record of Greek dancing can be found in the epic poems of Homer. One of the ancient Greeks' favorite muses was Terpsichore, the muse of dance. The syrtos is the most popular of all Greek line dances and is included on most traditional Greek albums. Hands are joined with the elbows bent. A scarf can be held between the first and second dancer. The line faces center, and the basic dance is as follows:

Step to the right.

Place the left foot behind the right—a quick step.

The right foot comes back so that the feet are together again.

Cross the left foot in front of the right foot and skip. This skipping step is done two more times.

Repeat by starting from the beginning.

Mount Olympus Alive, or the First Greek Olympics

Use this Olympics skit as a springboard for a performance given by the personas. Display Athene's quilt and other projects created by the students. Have the students go through the 12 Labors of Heracles. In the first Olympics, poets entertained the crowd between events, so make sure to display your students' poetry. The students may even recite their poems.

Characters:
- Achilles vs. Hermes
- Heracles vs. Atlas
- Jason vs. Ares
- Odysseus vs. Polyphemus the Cyclops
- Perseus vs. Medusa
- Theseus vs. Minotaur
- Apollo
- Hephaestus
- Hera
- Hestia
- Hippomenes
- Zeus

ZEUS: For as long as we can trace the civilization of ancient Greece, there was a great respect for the athlete. It was believed that mind and body needed discipline and that such a disciplined individual would honor me, Zeus.

HERA: To honor my husband, every four years, the Greeks would set everything aside, including war, to play in the Olympic Games—games that were named after our home, Mount Olympus.

HERMES: The first Olympic Games was nothing more than a 30-second foot race—a race I would surely have won with my winged sandals.

HEPHAESTUS: As god of the forge and of fire, I am here to light the Olympic torch.

HESTIA: If we were back at the original games, all the girls would have to leave. You see, in ancient Greece the games were part of a religious ceremony, and women were not allowed to watch.

APOLLO: Today you will witness some of the sports that were played during the early games. Back in those days, there were also musicians and poets performing between competitions. Since I am the god of music and poetry, those were my favorite parts.

ARES: There will be no music and poetry today, Apollo. In fact, you will notice that all the athletic events are military in nature. Face it, the best athlete was often the best warrior on the battlefield.

ZEUS: Enough with the talking. Bring on the heroes, and let the games begin!

(The gods all take their seats.)

HIPPOMENES: Being a runner, I'm happy to announce the first contest will be a footrace between the great hero Achilles and the winged messenger god, Hermes.

HERMES: I'm ready. I've been working out for centuries. So where is this guy?

ACHILLES: *(Limping onto the field)* Hermes, I can't race you today. I pulled my Achilles tendon. It's really a sad story. You see, when I was born, my mother wanted to make sure nothing bad would happen to me. She was told to dip me in the River Styx to protect me from harm. Unfortunately, when she dipped me, she held me by the heel, and that part didn't get wet. Now my only weakness is my Achilles' heel, and it had to flare up today of all days.

HIPPOMENES: Achilles forfeits! The laurel goes to Hermes!

HERA: The next competition is a contest in strength between the Titan Atlas and the hero Heracles.

ATLAS: Ever since I lost the war against the Olympian gods, Zeus has made me carry the world on my shoulders. It's been great weight training, but I'm about ready for someone else to carry the weight of the world on his shoulders.

HERACLES: What's up, Atlas? Besides the world, I mean. I was wondering if you could help me out. I'm in the middle of performing these labors, and I'm searching for some golden apples. I heard you know where they are.

ATLAS: I'd be happy to get them for you, Heracles—that is, if you could hoist the world on your shoulders for a few minutes. That is, if you're strong enough!

From *The Persona Book.* © 1997. Katherine Lallier and Nancy Marino. TIP. (800) 237-6124.

D. Spectacles: Mount Olympus Alive, or the First Greek Olympics

HERACLES: You deliver the apples, and I'll hold the world. Don't take too long! Gee, at this rate, maybe they'll name that book of maps a Heracles instead of an atlas.

ATLAS: I'm baaack! I've decided that I'll deliver the apples—you hold the world for a few centuries.

HERACLES: No problem—except I'd like to get a pad so that my shoulders don't ache. Could you take the world back while I put the pad on?

ATLAS: Sure. I should have done that ages ago myself.

HERACLES: Actually, you should have done it today. I'm going to deliver the apples myself.

HERA: Although he won by his brains more than his muscles, the laurel goes to the hero, Heracles!

HEPHAESTUS: I've been called the ugliest god, but wait until you get a look at Medusa as she does battle with Perseus. The athletic skill is sword fighting and not looking at Medusa.

MEDUSA: Perseus may be good with a sword, but all I have to do is get him to look at me. Then he'll turn to stone like all the rest of them!

PERSEUS: I just have to remember to look at her reflection in my shield. And not let her snake hair bite me!

(Sword fight. Perseus defeats Medusa.)

HEPHAESTUS: Perseus wins the laurel!

PERSEUS: Thanks, Athene. I couldn't have done it without you.

HESTIA: The next contest pits the Cyclops, Polyphemus, against the hero Odysseus. Let the javelin throw begin!

POLYPHEMUS THE CYCLOPS: Ever since that darn Odysseus threw a javelin in my eye, I've been waiting to get back at him. Thank you, Zeus, for returning my sight for this occasion.

From *The Persona Book*. © 1997. Katherine Lallier and Nancy Marino. TIP. (800) 237-6124.

Cyclops with javelin. [Left to right, Jennifer Berman, Jennifer Tobin, and Justine Boccia.]

ZEUS: Don't mention it. Just don't forget the sacrifice after you are done.

ODYSSEUS: I hope my lord Zeus will not be playing favorites just because the Cyclops gave you your first thunderbolt!

ZEUS: That is for me to know and you to find out, mortal!

(Javelin contest between the two.)

HESTIA: The laurel goes to Odysseus by a nose. Or should I say eye?

HERA: The wrestling match is between Theseus and the Minotaur. Sorry about not having a labyrinth for you to wrestle in.

THESEUS: Good Queen Hera, I will win this match for you. I will also do it in memory of all the young Athenians who this monster has devoured over the years!

MINOTAUR: You're no match for me, Theseus!

From *The Persona Book.* © 1997. Katherine Lallier and Nancy Marino. TIP. (800) 237-6124.

D. Spectacles: Mount Olympus Alive, or the First Greek Olympics   77

(The two wrestle with the Minotaur almost winning.)

HERA: Theseus is the victor! The laurel goes to him.

THESEUS: And this time I'll make sure the sail is white when I sail back home to see my father. The last time when he saw a black sail he thought I was dead, and that caused a lot of unnecessary trouble.

ZEUS: The final contest is my favorite: the chariot race. The race will be between the god of war, Ares, and the great hero of the Argonauts, Jason. Let the race begin!

ARES: You must think awfully well of yourself if you think you can beat a god! I'd say it borders on hubris!

JASON: I had a lot of chariot-racing experience when I was seeking the Golden Fleece. Anyway, Ares, not even your own wife, Aphrodite, likes you!

APOLLO: Gentlemen, start your horses!

(The race is a close one with Jason beating Ares.)

APOLLO: The laurel goes to Jason! *(To Jason)* I'd watch your back if I were you. Ares is a sore loser.

JASON: Thank you for the warning, Apollo. I'll be sure I make a burned sacrifice to you when I return to my ship, the Argo.

ZEUS: And so conclude the Olympic Games. We will meet again in four years. Before we conclude the festival, though, I have some unfinished business.

I am sure you all remember Prometheus. He's the Titan I had tied to a rock when he stole fire for mankind. I sort of feel bad about doing that to him. After all, without his little clay people, there would be no Olympics, no holy fires to honor us, no stories to tell or mischief to make. Heracles, come here. Prove your strength, and break the chains of Prometheus. He deserves to be free.

HERACLES: As you wish, great Zeus.

(Heracles releases Prometheus. Prometheus shakes hands with Zeus.)

From *The Persona Book.* © 1997. Katherine Lallier and Nancy Marino. TIP. (800) 237-6124.

PROMETHEUS: Thank-you, Zeus. My little clay people may not all be wonderful. Some stole and some argued, some were conceited and proud, but there were heroes and heroines among those men and women. I'm glad their stories could be told today.

Aphrodite awards laurel. [Laura Laccetti and Justine Boccia.]

Bibliography

Aliki. *The Gods and Goddesses of Olympus*. New York: HarperCollins, 1994.

Baker, Charles, and Rosalie Baker. *Myths and Legends of Mount Olympus*. New York: Cobblestone, 1994.

Birrer, Cynthia, and William Birrer. *Song to Demeter*. New York: Lothrop, Lee & Shepard, 1987.

Caselli, Giovanni. *Gods, Men and Monsters from the Greek Myths*. New York: Peter Bedrick Books, 1977.

Climo, Shirley. *Atalanta's Race: A Greek Myth*. New York: Clarion Books, 1995.

Fisher, Leonard Everett. *Cyclops*. New York: Holiday House, 1991.

———. *Jason and the Golden Fleece*. New York: Holiday House, 1990.

———. *The Olympians: Great Gods and Goddesses of Ancient Greece*. New York: Holiday House, 1984.

Ganeri, Anita. *Focus on Ancient Greeks*. New York: Shooting Star Press, 1993.

Hodges, Margaret. *The Arrow and the Lamp: The Story of Psyche*. Boston: Little, Brown, 1989.

Hutton, Warwick. *Perseus*. New York: Margaret K. McElderry Books, 1993.

———. *Theseus and the Minotaur*. New York: Margaret K. McElderry Books, 1989.

———. *The Trojan Horse*. New York: Margaret K. McElderry Books, 1992.

Low, Alice. *The Macmillan Book of Greek Gods and Heroes*. New York: Macmillan, 1985.

Martin, Claire. *The Race of the Golden Apples*. New York: Dial Books for Young Readers, 1991.

McCaughrean, Geraldine. *Greek Myths*. New York: Margaret K. McElderry Books, 1993.

Oldfield, Pamela. *Tales from Ancient Greece*. New York: Doubleday, 1988.

Orgel, Doris. *Ariadne, Awake!* New York: Viking, 1994.

Rockwell, Anne. *The Robber Baby: Stories from the Greek Myths*. New York: Greenwillow Books, 1994.

Waldherr, Kris. *Persephone and the Pomegranate: A Myth from Greece*. New York: Dial Books for Young Readers, 1993.

Williams, Marcia. *Greek Myths for Young Children*. Cambridge, Mass.: Candlewick Press, 1991.

Yolen, Jane. *Wings*. San Diego, Calif.: Harcourt Brace Jovanovich, 1991.

Software

Recess in Greece. CD-ROM; IBM 486 or better. Morgan Interactive, San Francisco, Calif.

3 Valley of the Kings

Discovering Ancient Egypt Through Its Mythology

Table of Contents

The Personas of Ancient Egypt	82
Step One: Prepersona Activities	86
Step Two: Decision Making	87
Step Three: Discovery Period	88
Culminating Activities	93
A. Dramas	93
B. Activities and Games	102
C. Displays	107
D. Spectacles	110
Bibliography	114

Valley of the Kings

On the west bank of the great Nile River, opposite the New Kingdom capital of Thebes, lies the royal burial ground called the Valley of the Kings. Buried under the sands of time is the splendor that was ancient Egypt. In 1922, the greatest archaeological discovery of our time was uncovered: the tomb of Tutankhamen. The opulence surrounding the boy king's burial chamber fueled curiosity about this marvelous civilization. More than any other culture, ancient Egypt is a natural wonder to students who study bygone civilizations. The magnificent wealth of the pharaohs, the eerie half-human, half-animal gods and goddesses, the practice of mummification, and the hints of deadly curses afflicting the tomb robbers stagger the most potent imagination. The following unit seeks to combine all of these ingredients into the study of ancient Egypt. Using the personas of Egyptian gods as well as the historical personalities of pharaohs and twentieth century archaeologists, students will develop a personal connection with and appreciation for this unique civilization.

There is a treasure trove of activities provided in this unit for you to develop and explore. It is not recommended that you do everything unless you have unlimited time to spend on a unit. Choose a select number of activities that appeal to you and suit the needs of your students. Creating your own Rosetta stone to accompany the hieroglyphic scavenger hunt is a terrific way to enrich your study of ancient Egypt. Concentrating on the archaeological dig that unearthed Tutankhamen or the dramatization of making your own mummy will enthrall young Egyptologists. Whatever activities you choose to do will allow students to experience ancient Egypt in a unique and enriching way.

The Personas of Ancient Egypt

The purpose of this persona list is to easily identify the main characters of Egyptian history and mythology. The sketches are brief and can be used as a reminder to students and teachers involved in Valley of the Kings. Some of the mythological gods and goddesses have minimal information available on a juvenile level. There are several excellent books—including Harris's *Gods and Pharaohs from Egyptian Mythology* and Reeves's *Into the Mummy's Tomb: The Real-Life Discovery of Tutankhamen's Treasures*—that were used to create the sketches of the personas in the list below. Students can look to these books for information on their personas. The books in which each persona can be found are referred to in the subheadings of the list below. Many of these characters are historical, so instead of looking at the mythology, students can look to Egyptian history books for information about their personas. This list will be used in conjunction with the decision-making lesson.

Egyptian names do not clearly identify gender. Therefore, an asterisk (*) in front of a name denotes a role for a girl.

Pharaohs

The following personas are taken directly from the history books. Because there is a wealth of information available on the great pharaohs of Egypt, only brief sketches are offered here.

Akhenaten: Husband of Nefertiti. He banished all the Egyptian gods except the sun god, Aten. After his death, his successor restored the gods and their temples. His name became hated, and his temples were torn down.

*Ankhesenamun: King Tut's wife. The pair were very much in love but did not yet have any children. When Tut died, she tried to marry another young man, but he was murdered.

*Cleopatra: Married to the pharaoh, Ptolemy, she was the last in a line of Greek rulers in Egypt. She supposedly committed suicide by allowing herself to be bitten by a snake called an asp.

*Hatshepsut: The only true woman pharaoh, she ruled for about 20 years.

Khufu: The Sphinx at Giza was carved to protect his pyramid. He lived 4,500 years ago.

*Nefertiti: The wife of Akhenaten, she helped her husband set up a cult to the sun god, Aten.

Pepy II: Reigned as pharaoh for 94 years. He holds the record for the longest reign of any monarch.

Ramses II: Ramses the Great reigned over Egypt for 67 years. He built more monuments and statues than any other pharaoh.

Tutankhamen: This ruler died at 18 from mysterious circumstances. His tomb was discovered in 1922 and was the greatest archaeological find ever.

Tuthmosis IV: This king became famous because he freed the great Sphinx at Giza from the sand that had blown around it. The cobra goddess he wears on his head protects him by spitting out instant death to any enemy. Only pharaohs and queens could wear the cobra.

Archaeologists

An exciting children's account of the discovery of the tomb of Tutankhamen is provided in Reeves's *Into the Mummy's Tomb: The Real-Life Discovery of Tutankhamen's Treasures*. Information on Lord Carnarvon and Howard Carter are widely available, but the lesser-known characters are all referred to in Reeves's book.

Howard Carter: Discovered the tomb of Tutankhamen in 1922. He was an Egyptologist as well as an artist. His life work was to find Tut's tomb, then he spent the following 10 years overseeing the excavation.

Lord Carnarvon: Financed the expedition to find Tut. He died four months after the discovery of Tut. His death was attributed to the mummy's curse.

Gods and Goddesses

Harris's *Gods and Pharaohs from Egyptian Mythology* is an essential anthology when studying the deities of ancient Egypt. The following personas can be found in this one source unless otherwise noted.

Anubis: The son of Set and Nephtys, he was represented as a black jackal and was a god of the dead and mummification. He protected the dead and brought them to Osiris to be judged. He was always present at the embalming and acted as guardian of the cemeteries.

Aten: At first, this sun god was considered a minor god, but he was raised to the position of supreme god by the pharaoh, Akhenaten.

*Bast (Bastet): The cat goddess, Bast represented the gentle fertilizing warmth of the Nile Valley and was responsible for bringing sunlight to the Earth.

Bes: A dwarflike god who wore lion skins and protected the home and children. He was ugly but happy and joyful. He protected ordinary Egyptians against evil omens and animals and was the god of music, dance, and feasting.

Chonsu (Knons): Son of Mut, he was the moon god. He had great healing powers and wore a crescent moon on a skullcap. He was represented as handsome and strong. The pharaohs prayed to him for their power.

Geb: This Earth god was also the father of Osiris, Isis, Set, and Nephtys. He is much like the Greek Cronus and usually has a goose head. He was ruler of the Earth until his son, Osiris, succeeded him.

Hapi: He was the god of the Nile and caused the river to flood every year. He was one of the four sons of Osiris who watched over the canopic jars, the jars that held a mummy's vital organs. He had the head of an ape.

*Hathor: This goddess was like the Greek Aphrodite. She protected women and was the goddess of love. She also protected the dead and welcomed them with bread and water. When Ra sent her to punish mankind, she changed into the war-loving Sekhmet.

Horus: The son of Isis and Osiris, he grew up to avenge the murder of his father. He is often represented as a falcon.

*Isis: The wife of Osiris and the mother of Horus. Isis was known as the mistress of magic. She often wears brightly colored wings. Isis is the eldest daughter of Nut and Geb.

Khnum (Khnemu): Lord of the upper river and the Nile cataracts. He created humans from clay at his potter's wheel. He is often shown with a ram's head.

*Maat: Maat is a mother goddess and goddess of justice, truth, and the law. She was the daughter of Ra and the mistress of the gods. She always wears an ostrich feather, because a feather was the symbol of truth. When she weighed the heart of a dead man, a feather would be placed in the other pan of the scale.

*Mertseger: The silent cobra goddess protected the Valley of the Kings. She was well known in the city of Thebes as a punisher of evil with her deadly, venomous bite.

Mont (Menthu): War god who battled the enemies of the pharaoh. Sometimes he has a bull head, other times he wears a falcon head. He is similar to the Greek Apollo. His sacred bull was Buchis, and some thought it possessed the soul of Ra.

*Mut: The goddess of motherhood, Mut was the wife of Amun and an important goddess. She was sometimes known as the queen of heaven. She wore the vulture cap of queens. When Akhenaten tried to eliminate Amun as an object of worship, Mut suffered the same fate.

*Nehmauit: Wife of Thoth. Her name means uprooter of evil.

*Neith: The goddess who was like the Greek Athene. She represented femininity. She was a warrior goddess and a skilled weaver. Some believe Neith wove the world. She protected the dead and the mummified bodies that were awaiting burial.

*Nephtys: Her name means mistress of the house. She was the wife of Set, the mother of Anubis, the sister of Isis, and the daughter of Nut and Geb. Nephtys was a loyal and gentle character who disliked her husband intensely. At the judging of the dead, she stands behind Osiris.

Nunu (Nun): The ocean god from which the world was shaped, Nunu existed at the beginning of time before the universe was created. The god Ra emerged from the chaos that was Nunu, thus he was known as the father of the gods.

*Nut: This sky goddess was the wife of the Earth god, Geb, and the mother of Isis, Osiris, Set, and Nephtys as well as the stars. She is compared to the Greek goddess Rhea. She holds up the sky and is either depicted as a cow or a woman holding a vase on her head.

Osiris: This god of the dead was at one time the king of Egypt. He was the oldest of five children born to Nut and Geb. He took his sister, Isis, as his queen. Osiris ruled wisely and was greatly loved. His evil brother killed him and tore his body to pieces. Osiris became the first Egyptian mummy.

Ptah: Known as the creator of the universe, Ptah is represented as a man wearing a beard and robe and holding a scepter. He is the oldest of all Egyptian gods and is known as the highest leader of art and craftsmen.

Ra (Ra-Atum): The most famous of all Egyptian gods, Ra was the sun and the source of life. All pharaohs were known as the son of Ra, and his name was attached to theirs. Ra is also the father of Shu and Tefenet. He is usually represented by a falcon head with a sun on top.

*Sati: Wife of Khnum who preyed on the dead. She helped her husband Khnum protect the Nile. She wears a white crown with two horns and holds a bow and arrow.

Sebek (Sobek): Crocodile god who represented all of the pharaohs and their power. Sanctuaries were built to honor him, and many sacrifices were made in his name because he was considered to be evil. He is the god of rivers and lakes where crocodiles dwell.

*Sekhmet: The wife of Ptah, this lion-headed goddess represented the desert. She is a warrior goddess who protected Ra and destroyed his enemies. Originally, she was the love goddess, Hathor, but became the warrior goddess when Ra sent her to punish mankind.

Set (Seth): The evil god who strove to undo all the good accomplished by his brother, Osiris. He would have succeeded in his brother's absence were it not for Isis. Set was regarded as the lord of the deserts and the god of war and violence. The younger son of Nut and Geb, he married his sister, Nephtys.

Thoth: The ibis-headed god was in charge of wisdom, knowledge, and magic. He invented all arts and sciences and was known as a record keeper because he invented writing. Thoth was created by Ra but played a trick on him to help Nut give birth to her children. In the afterlife, he reads the scales as the souls of the dead are weighed.

Weneg: The scribe of Ra. Scribes were important in Egyptian society. Everything was written down on papyrus and taxed for the pharaoh and local gods. Scribes are always shown sitting cross-legged with a scroll between their knees.

Other Mortals

Jean-François Champollion: In the early nineteenth century, he figured out how to read the hieroglyphs of the ancient Egyptians. He discovered that the symbols used did not stand for letters or sounds but for people and ideas.

Imhotep: A famous architect and scribe during the Third Dynasty. He designed the oldest pyramid. His fame continued generation after generation until he was considered a god. He is known as the son of Ptah and the patron of doctors and scribes.

Rhodopis: A Greek slave girl who lived nearly 2,000 years ago, her remains were discovered in one of the great pyramids. It is said that she became the wife of a pharaoh when he discovered her shoe and wanted to know its owner. Today she is also known as the Egyptian Cinderella. Climo's *The Egyptian Cinderella* is a detailed retelling of this folktale.

Step One: Prepersona Activities

1. Compared to Greek mythology, there are relatively few books on Egyptian mythology available for children. There is an excellent anthology by Harris, *Gods and Pharaohs from Egyptian Mythology*, that will prove invaluable. However, this project takes a great deal from actual history, and there are many wonderful nonfiction books on ancient Egypt that you will want to share with your class.

Besides the Harris anthology, some excellent read-aloud books to introduce children to the wonders of ancient Egypt are Sabuda's *Tutankhamen's Gift*, Aliki's *Mummies Made in Egypt*, and even primary picture books such as Gerrard's *Croco'nile*, and dePaola's *Bill and Pete Go Down the Nile*. There are exciting novels for children relating to the subject, including Dexter's *The Gilded Cat*, and Karr's *Gideon and the Mummy Professor*. Snyder's *The Egypt Game* is a terrific whole-class book. There are general mythology collections, such as Hamilton's *In the Beginning: Creation Stories Around the World*, which offer the creation myth about the god Ra. There are supernatural tales that touch on the mummy's curse, such as "The Tale of Joshua Something," included in McDonald's *Nightwaves: Scary Tales for After Dark*. The famous Tutankhamen expedition is recounted in many sources, including Reeves's *Into the Mummy's Tomb: The Real-Life Discovery of Tutankhamen's Treasures*. There is no shortage of reading when you begin your ancient Egyptian unit of study.

2. Start to introduce ancient Egypt. Persona-based enrichment provides many avenues for learning about ancient Egypt; however, you may want to provide some background. Topics that might be covered are the pyramids, mummies, the Nile, town life, and the life of the pharaohs.

3. Develop a strategy to introduce children to role playing: Read the story of "Isis and Osiris." A version of this story may be found in Harris's *Gods and Pharaohs from Egyptian Mythology*. There is also a picture-book version available in McDermott's *The Voyage of Osiris: A Myth of Ancient Egypt*. Ask the children to reenact the story by role-playing the characters of Set, Isis, Osiris, and Nephtys. A skit of this story is included in this chapter.

    To encourage children to start thinking in the first person, ask them the following questions. Their responses may be written or oral.

    A. What if you were Set? How would you feel about your brother being king and your sister being queen? Why did Set have to kill his brother so brutally?

    B. What if you were Nephtys? How would you feel about your husband's violent actions?

    C. What if you were Isis? How would you feel about your brother and your husband? Would you search for your husband's body?

Step Two: Decision Making

When students have been introduced to some of the myths, legends, and history of ancient Egypt, the persona element can be introduced.

1. Explain to students that they will be choosing a persona and doing projects as that persona. Talk about some of the culminating projects. Explain that there are different types of projects and that each of them will be taking part in several. Explain as well that some of the characters will be involved in performances while others will be managing and organizing activities.

2. Ask each student to choose three personas and give reasons why he or she wants to be this character. These reasons will be important if two or more children want to be the same persona.

3. Place the list of the "Valley of the Kings" criteria for decision making in a visible place, and give each student a copy. Encourage them to invent additional criteria. See pages 89-90 for a copy of the decision-making form.

4. Review the list of personas, and emphasize the lesser-known characters. Have a list of personas for the students to refer to when choosing.

5. Explain that, in addition to specific personas, a student can opt to create a persona. For example, if a student wishes to become a scribe, a common slave, or a vizier, she then needs to create a name and a personal history.

6. Have students complete the "Valley of the Kings Decision-Making Work Sheet."

7. As part of the lesson that follows, have a conference with each student individually. It is especially important to talk with students who did not get their first choice, because everyone should be happy with their choices.

Step Three: Discovery Period

During this time, students delve into ancient Egypt. While they should be encouraged to collect information about their personas, the primary purpose of this unit is to explore ancient Egypt. Library time is discovery time. Students examine books, CD-ROMs, encyclopedias, online sources, and other avenues of information. Many CD-ROMs are available on ancient Egypt, including *Annabel's Dream of Ancient Egypt*, by Texas Caviar Inc.; *Secrets of the Pyramids*, by Highsmith; *Nile Passage to Egypt*, by Discovery Channel Multimedia; and *The Egyptian Pyramids*, by InterOptica. Every classroom lesson gives more information about how their personas lived and behaved. Students can create persona journals that are written in the first person and include answers to questions.

Questions for Gods and Goddesses

Describe your personality.

What was your physical appearance?

What did the ancient Egyptians believe you could do that made you so important?

What did ancient Egyptians believe Egypt would be like without you?

Is there something in nature for which you are responsible?

Describe a typical ancient-Egyptian follower? What was he or she like? How did he or she live?

Name _____

VALLEY OF THE KINGS
DECISION-MAKING WORK SHEET

DECISION: WHICH PERSONA DO I WANT TO BECOME FOR THE VALLEY OF THE KINGS?

Below is a list of some of your choices:

1. Pharaohs or Historical Figures

2. Twentieth Century Archaeologists

3. Gods and Goddesses

4. A Personal Creation: Scribe, Slave, etc.

Answer the questions on the following page. Use your answers to make a decision, and give reasons for that decision. The better your answer, the more likely it is that you will receive your choice. List two alternatives.

Give three choices in order of preference.

1. _____

2. _____

3. _____

From *The Persona Book*. © 1997. Katherine Lallier and Nancy Marino. TIP. (800) 237-6124.

Name _____

VALLEY OF THE KINGS
DECISION-MAKING WORK SHEET
Page 2

DECISION: WHICH PERSONA DO I WANT TO BECOME FOR THE VALLEY OF THE KINGS?

1. Why do I want to be this persona?

2. What do I like about the persona of the character?

3. Do I want to have a big part in the performance?

4. Will I do extra research concerning this character?

5. Will I be able to design and make the costume?

From *The Persona Book.* © 1997. Katherine Lallier and Nancy Marino. TIP. (800) 237-6124.

Questions for Mortals and Historical Figures

Where did you live?	What was a typical day like?
What did you like to eat?	What did you wear?
What was your status in society?	What dangers did you face?
What was your job?	Will you be buried in a pyramid?
What did you do for fun?	

Take Your Persona Down the Nile

What was the Nile like during ancient times?

What is the Nile like today?

Compare and contrast the two Niles, being certain to consider the different sights along the Nile. Be sure to include the natural world—landscape, plants, and animals—as well as man-made sights. What are the pros and cons of the modern and ancient worlds? For the comparison, students can create a Venn diagram.

Personas may report on various topics. Below is a list of possible topics that certain types of personas can pursue.

Pharaohs
The life of a royal in Egypt

Town life in Egypt

Archaeologists
Pyramids

Treasures in the tomb, jewelry, and adornment

Gods and Goddesses
Mummies

Mythology in Egypt

Mortals
The Nile

The Rosetta stone and ancient hieroglyphics

Who Am I?

The "Who Am I?" work sheet (see page 92), encourages children to create a page for the "Persona Pyramid." This is one of the important culminating activities. Writing is one of the most difficult tasks that students are asked to do. A blank piece of paper can be intimidating—especially in regard to creative writing. This questionnaire is provided to ease the students into the writing process. The results, written in the first person, will be included on their page in the "Persona Pyramid." The children will also design a picture of their personas to accompany the creative writing.

Student's Name _____

Persona's Name _____

VALLEY OF THE KINGS WHO AM I? WORK SHEET

Whether your persona comes from Egyptian mythology, royalty, recent history, or is a character you are creating, you must let everyone know who you are. In no fewer than seven sentences, tell me about yourself. Be sure to include some of the information from your journals.

Examples of what you might include are:

1. What is your job or purpose?

2. Do you have any talents or special powers?

3. Tell a story about yourself.

4. Are you related to anyone else in ancient Egypt?

5. What kind of dangers do you face?

6. How would you describe yourself—shy, brave, mysterious, ruthless, wild, heroic, fearless, afraid, curious, obedient, confident, smart, dedicated, beautiful, romantic, loyal, humble, evil, honest, sly, or fair?

From *The Persona Book*. © 1997. Katherine Lallier and Nancy Marino. TIP. (800) 237-6124.

Culminating Activities

There are many exciting activities awaiting your pharaohs, archaeologists, and deities in "Valley of the Kings." The following events allow your students to share their personas' stories with everyone. "Valley of the Kings" is a collection of displays, demonstrations, and interactive happenings that center on the history and mythology of ancient Egypt.

Below are the types of culminating activities for this unit. Select as many activities as you will need for all your students to participate.

Dramas. If your students love the idea of putting on a play, choose some of the skits included in this chapter. Students should be encouraged to enhance and elaborate on the dramas provided or, better yet, to create their own.

Activities and Games. Use these activities if you want the entire school or just selected grade levels to participate in "Valley of the Kings." The personas who are listed for these activities should organize and manage the events, with the teacher taking on the role of adviser.

Displays. These art projects are the perfect way to transform your classroom, library, or auditorium into ancient Egypt.

Spectacles. These activities can be performed in front a large audience. They are usually favorites with participants and spectators alike.

A. Dramas

The following is a collection of performance scripts based on Egyptian mythology, history, and an actual archaeological discovery. Students should be encouraged to expand on the existing dramas or create their own. Stage instructions are minimal so that the students may direct themselves.

> The story of Isis and Osiris is perhaps the most famous of all the Egyptian myths. It explains the jealous rage of one evil brother and the devotion of a beloved spouse. It tells how Osiris became the first mummy and the god of the dead. The actual myth is much more detailed and has many more scenes, so feel free to adapt more of this great tale if needed.

The Myth of Osiris and Isis

Characters:
- Imhotep (or another character to act as narrator)
- Isis
- Mont
- Osiris
- Set
- Two to four henchmen
- Feast guests

Setting: At first, a simple chair for Osiris. At the party scene, you will need a table, glasses for toasting, and a large box (coffin) that Osiris can actually step into and be covered in.

ISIS: I'm worried, Osiris. Your brother Set will stop at nothing to gain your throne. I fear for your very life, my love.

OSIRIS: My beautiful, Isis. Please don't worry. Set is crafty, but he would never kill his king. The people of Egypt would never allow it. Besides, Set is nothing more than a coward.

ISIS: I do not trust him, Husband.

OSIRIS: He is our brother, Isis. He may not deserve our trust, but we must attend the feast he is giving in my honor. Who knows, maybe Set is changing his ways. Surely no one is all bad. Say no more on the subject for it is done.

(Exit Isis and Osiris. Enter Set and his henchmen.)

SET: This time I have him! The plan is going perfectly. That fool Osiris has already accepted my invitation to dinner. A feast for the deceased! Ha, ha, ha.

MONT: The coffin is finished, my lord. Will you tell me your plan now?

SET: At the end of this evening's festivities, I want you to bring out the coffin. I will tell my guests that it is a present to the guest who fits in it best.

From *The Persona Book.* © 1997. Katherine Lallier and Nancy Marino. TIP. (800) 237-6124.

MONT:	But the coffin was designed with Osiris' measurements in mind. It will naturally be given to . . . oh, I see, my lord.
SET:	I'm glad you figured it out, Mont. I'd hate to think I made you the god of war for nothing. Now put the coffin away until this evening. I still have much to do to prepare because after tonight, I will be king!

(Exit Set and Mont)

Scene: End of feast with many guests.

IMHOTEP:	A toast! To our gracious host, Set, who prepared this feast to honor our good king, Osiris.
ALL:	To Set!
SET:	You all honor me by being present in my humble home. I am so moved by you all being here that I've prepared a little surprise.
ISIS:	(*To Osiris*) Watch out, he's planning something now.
OSIRIS:	(*To Isis*) Set has been the perfect host all night. Can't we just trust that he has changed?
ISIS:	Your faith and goodness blind you, Osiris. Set is evil, and he means to kill you!
OSIRIS:	Enough, Isis.
ISIS:	Please be careful.
OSIRIS:	I said enough.
SET:	My dear guests, I present this beautiful box to you for your approval.
ALL:	Ahh!
SET:	As beautiful as it is, it's only one box and can therefore only go home with one of you. I've devised a little game to see who the winner will be. Mont, will you explain?
MONT:	Yes, my lord. The person who best fits in the box wins it. Step right up, and try it on for size.

From *The Persona Book*. © 1997. Katherine Lallier and Nancy Marino. TIP. (800) 237-6124.

SET: Maybe my lovely sister-in-law would like to be the first to try to win the box?

ISIS: I would never accept a gift from you, Set. I would rather be bitten by a cobra.

OSIRIS: Isis! My brother is doing his best. Set, may I be the first to try to win your box?

SET: As you wish, dear brother.

(Osiris steps in the box, which is nailed shut by Mont. The box is taken away by Mont and others.)

ISIS: *(Being held back)* Set, what are you doing? Osiris! Osiris!

SET: My dear, Isis. Osiris should have listened to you. When I make you my wife, I'll be sure to mind what you say—especially in regard to stepping into any boxes.

ISIS: What have you done with Osiris?

SET: By now, my men should be on their way to the town of Tanis. When they arrive, they will dispose of that box by throwing it into the Nile River. It's a shame to throw away such a beautiful box, but that's the price of becoming the new king.

ISIS: Let me go, Set. I must find Osiris. Without a proper burial, he will never rest in the land of the dead. *(Isis escapes)*

SET: Let her go. She'll never find him. I've had his body cut into 14 pieces and scattered to the four winds. Let her try to find him. She is destined to be my wife, and I am destined to be king, to be pharaoh of all Egypt.

IMHOTEP: The evil Set may have killed his brother, but he would not be rid of him so easily. Isis would eventually find the 14 pieces of her husband's body and bind them in yards of linen. Osiris, who was the king of the land of the dead, would become the first Egyptian mummy.

From *The Persona Book.* © 1997. Katherine Lallier and Nancy Marino. TIP. (800) 237-6124.

> Cinderella is the most common folktale in the world. It has variants in every country, and Egypt is no exception. It has been recorded that more than 2,000 years ago a Greek slave girl named Rhodopis actually rose to become the wife of a pharaoh. An eagle mysteriously dropped Rhodopis's slipper into the pharaoh's lap, and he became intrigued enough to want to find the owner. For a lovely retelling of this tale, read Climo's *The Egyptian Cinderella*, with beautiful illustrations by Ruth Heller. For a dramatic, poetic rendition of the tale, use the following poem, which may be recited by one or two students. Use first person if Rhodopis tells her own rags-to-riches tale.

The Egyptian Cinderella

In the land of Egypt,
where the green Nile flows
There is a story
that everyone knows.

About a lovely young slave
whose family was Greek
Who was green-eyed and blond
and red in the cheek.

Her name was Rhodopis,
but the servant girls teased
Taunting her with names
she'd fall to her knees.

Her master was kind
He bestowed her with gifts
And so the servant girls
began having fits.

Rhodopis was given slippers
Fashioned from gold
The servant girls grew angry
So brazenly bold

They worked poor Rhodopis
With chore after chore
The slave girl grew tired
And prayed for no more.

An announcement soon came
Of the pharaoh's fine feast
The servant girls assured Rhodopis
She'd be welcome the least

The others set sail
Leaving Rhodopis behind
She had linen to wash
And grain to grind.

As she worked
A great eagle descended
Who was this bird
Whom Rhodopis befriended?

The eagle saw her slippers
And took one in the sky
Rhodopis beckoned him back
But it ignored her cry.

From *The Persona Book*. © 1997. Katherine Lallier and Nancy Marino. TIP. (800) 237-6124.

He flew over the Nile
To the feast of the pharaoh
He bode his time
His great eyes did narrow.

He then dropped the slipper
For the pharaoh to find
The pharaoh exclaimed,
"The gods have sent me a sign!"

In a matter of moments
The slipper was seen
As a way to find
The pharaoh's royal queen

The search took him all over
Up and down the Nile
He tried the slipper on everyone
None made him smile

The pharaoh finally arrived
At the home of Rhodopis
Would the slipper fit anyone?
It seemed to be hopeless.

The servant girls claimed
That the slipper was theirs
Each tried it on
And the others all stared.

So upset was the pharaoh
He decided to quit
Then Rhodopis tried on the slipper
For a perfect fit.

"Behold, queen of Egypt!"
The pharaoh did say
But the servant girls insisted
"She's merely a slave!"

"She is a true Egyptian,"
The pharaoh did smile,
"Her face is as fair as good Isis
Her eyes, green as the Nile."

She lived happily ever after
As Cinderellas do
But what makes this tale different—
Her story is true.

The following rap was researched and created by Marie Shea, a sixth-grade teacher at the Robert W. Carbonaro School, Valley Stream, New York.

The Pharaoh Rap

Characters:
Hatshepsut   *Ramses*
Khufu   *Tutankhamen*
Nefertiti

Setting: Each pharaoh is standing in front of a sarcophagus facade. They are sleeping until it is their turn to speak.

ALL: Welcome to the valley,
The Valley of the Kings.

Listen very closely
And you'll learn so many things

You'll hear of life in ancient Egypt
Fascinating facts and mysteries. . .

The pharaoh kings and royal queens
Awake to share their histories. . .

KHUFU: I am the pharaoh Khufu
And here is my claim to fame. . .
I ordered a pyramid constructed
That puts all others to shame

With meager tools of ropes and chisels
My servants diligently honed
A 500-foot-high pyramid
Made of 2 million blocks of stone

I taxed my people mercilessly
In order to build my shrine
People still marvel at my great pyramid
And its phenomenal design.

From *The Persona Book.* © 1997. Katherine Lallier and Nancy Marino. TIP. (800) 237-6124.

HATSHEPSUT: Please greet the royal Hatshepsut

ALL: "God bless you!"
That was no sneeze. That's my name!
I was the one true female pharaoh,
Quite unusual for a dame!

I was assigned initially as a regent
For the young Thutmose (he was next in line);
But after seven years of advising,
I declared the role of pharaoh as mine.

I wore the customary robe,
Upon my face was the ceremonial beard.
Trade flourished under my leadership,
For two decades I was revered.

NEFERTITI: Behold, I am Queen Nefertiti;
My name implies great beauty.
My husband Akhenaten and I
Made sun worshipping our duty.

Before we began our reign,
Praying to many gods was tradition.
But we gave the great sun
The highest of all positions.

In reliefs depicting our family,
We are very happily shown.
We had several lovely daughters,
But no male to inherit the throne.

Akhenaten did have a son,
Conceived by another wife.
It was he who became the king
When Akhenaten lost his life.

His name was Tutankhamen
And he was not even 10 years old;
Yet he did become the pharaoh,
He was wise, and he was bold.

From *The Persona Book*. © 1997. Katherine Lallier and Nancy Marino. TIP. (800) 237-6124.

A. Dramas: The Pharaoh Rap

TUTANKHAMEN: My name is Tutankhamen
(King Tut I'm called for short).
At the age of nine years old
I was pharaoh, king of the court.

As king I soon decided
To end the silly worship of the sun.
I reinstated all other gods;
This seemed to please everyone.

By 19 years of age,
I had passed into the afterlife.
My death is still a mystery;
They suspect I was murdered by knife.

A man named Howard Carter
And his archaeological crew
Made the discovery of my burial site
In the year 1922.

They were amazed and overjoyed
At the contents of my tomb.
There was jewelry, furniture, and chariots
And my golden coffin in another room.

RAMSES: I am the mighty Ramses
And for 67 years did I reign.
I built so many statues of myself,
Some thought I was extremely vain.

I fought a great many battles
In order to regain my land.
I made peace lasting 50 years
For this don't I deserve a hand?

(Pharaohs applaud.)

I'll share with you something amazing—
(There's no doubt that these facts are true)
I had hundreds of wives and more than 900 kids,
More than that old lady who lived in a shoe!

From *The Persona Book*. © 1997. Katherine Lallier and Nancy Marino. TIP. (800) 237-6124.

ALL: So now you've heard the stories,
They've been shared so graciously.

We're sure they have awakened
An ancient-Egyptian curiosity.

There's so much more information
About ancient-Egyptian days

Keep searching for more details
Of our intriguing ways. . .

Go now from the valley,
So that the kings and queens may rest.

Tell others what you've learned here,
Put your knowledge to the test!

From *The Persona Book*. © 1997. Katherine Lallier and Nancy Marino. TIP. (800) 237-6124.

B. Activities and Games

The following two activities require participation on the part of other classes or the entire school. These activities should be the responsibility of the personas who did not wish to have a speaking part in the more formalized drama or spectacle.

The Search for the Sacred Scarab of Ramses II: A Scavenger Hunt

This scavenger hunt can be adapted for the entire school, a grade level, or your own class. It can be done over a period of days or in a single afternoon. The final hiding place of the "sacred beetle," or scarab, can be in the library or classroom. The clues ultimately lead students to look under the teacher's chair for the scarab, which should be securely taped underneath.

This activity is a perfect vehicle for the persona of Jean-François Champollion, the Frenchman who solved the mystery of the Rosetta stone and Egyptian hieroglyphics. Champollion and some scribes can organize the scavenger hunt by using the model provided or creating their own scavenger hunt.

This scavenger hunt can be expanded or used as a simple exercise in code ciphering.

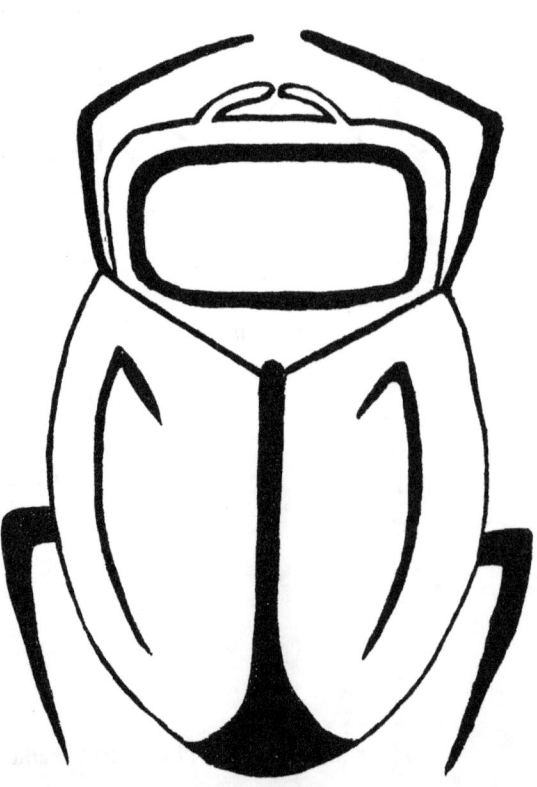

THE HIEROGLYPHIC ALPHABET
FOR BREAKING THE CODE

A B C D E

F G H I J K

L M N O P

Q R S T U V

W X Y Z

From *The Persona Book*. © 1997. Katherine Lallier and Nancy Marino. TIP. (800) 237-6124.

THE SEARCH FOR THE SACRED SCARAB

The sacred scarab of Ramses II is missing! It must be found quickly so that it can be included in the mummy of the departed pharaoh. All the scribes of Egypt must unite to break the code and find the missing amulet. The finder of the sacred scarab will be justly rewarded by Osiris in the afterlife. Good luck!

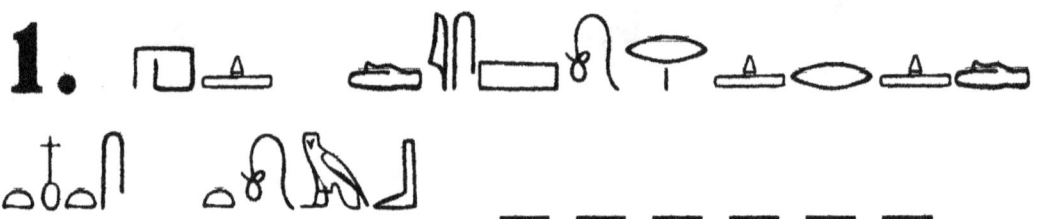

1.

2.

3.

4.

From *The Persona Book*. © 1997. Katherine Lallier and Nancy Marino. TIP. (800) 237-6124.

5.

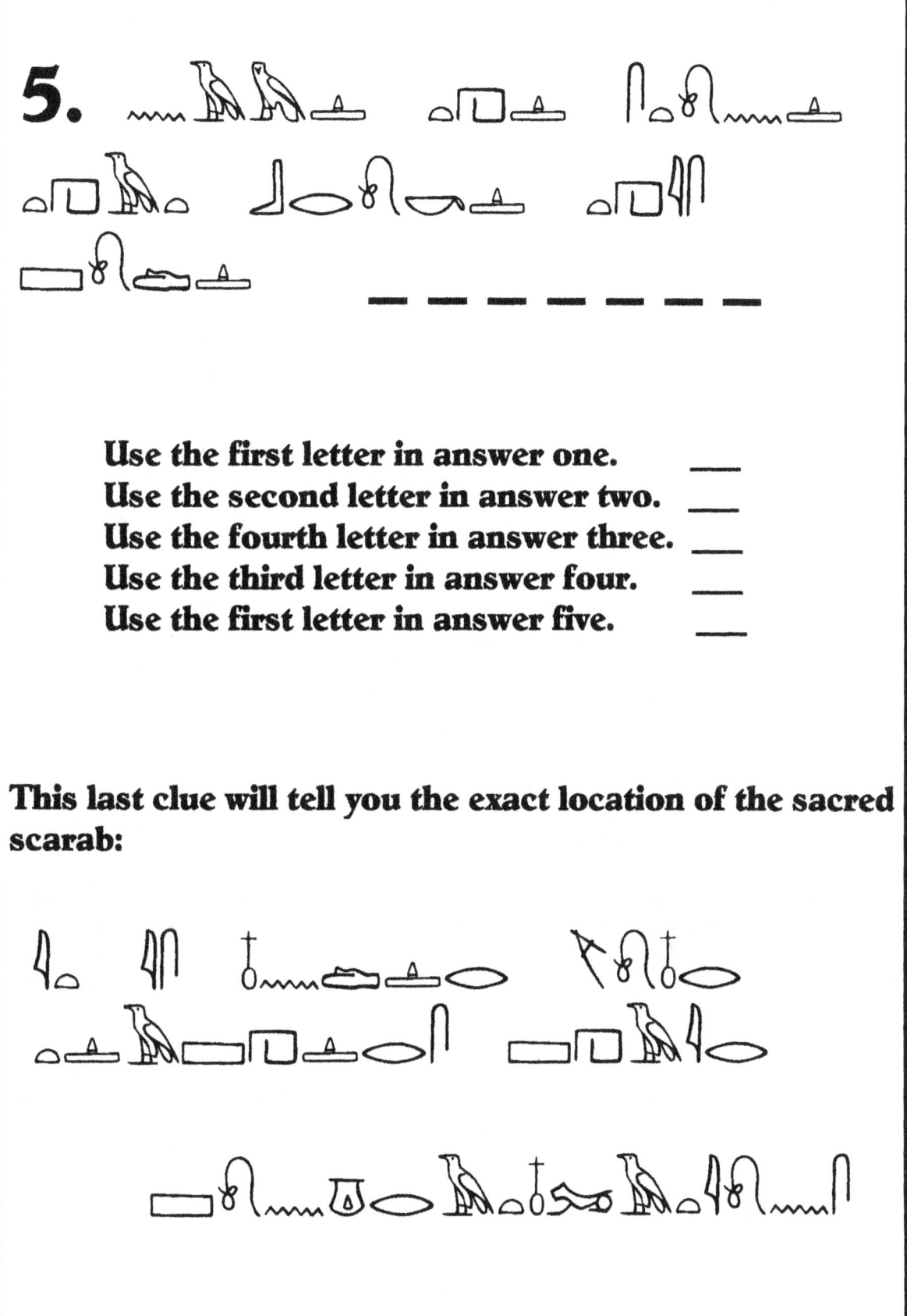

Use the first letter in answer one. ___
Use the second letter in answer two. ___
Use the fourth letter in answer three. ___
Use the third letter in answer four. ___
Use the first letter in answer five. ___

This last clue will tell you the exact location of the sacred scarab:

Below is the answer key for "The Sacred Scarab of Ramses II: A Scavenger Hunt."

> 1. He discovered Tut's tomb. **CARTER**
> 2. Egyptian kings. **PHARAOHS**
> 3. Pharaohs were buried in these buildings. **PYRAMIDS**
> 4. Husband of Isis. **OSIRIS**
> 5. Name the stone that broke this code. **ROSETTA**
>
> The hiding place is *chair*.
> The last clue in hieroglyphics says:
>
> **It is under your teacher's chair.**
>
> *Congratulations!*

Persona Puzzles

Use a crossword-puzzle-maker software package, such as *Crossword Magic*, by Mindscape/SVE. Have students create their own crosswords. Students choose the words and their definitions, and the software makes the puzzle. Creating short definitions for words helps reinforce students' knowledge of the content area. Students enjoy solving each other's puzzles.

The 10,000-Deben Pyramid With Your Host, Thoth

This game can be an interactive crowd pleaser with your "Valley of the Kings" audience or a simple review game for your class.

Thoth, the ibis-headed god of wisdom, knowledge, and magic, is a logical host for your game show. Nehmauit, wife of Thoth, can also be involved in organizing this activity.

The *deben* in the title of the show refers to the unit of measure ancient Egyptians used in bargaining and trading. The object of the game is to spell *pyramid* by correctly answering questions. Each correct answer earns the player a letter to spell *pyramid*.

Your contestants will determine the question's level of difficulty. If it is simply a review game for your class, your questions will be more difficult than the ones provided here. These questions were designed for contestants with little or no prior knowledge of ancient Egypt. The questions have been gleaned from the performances.

Your students can work in teams of three or four. The student who plays Thoth can host this game by asking each team a question. For each correct answer, Thoth awards the team a letter. The first team to spell the word *pyramid* wins.

Following are some sample questions for the game.

1. True or False: King Tut was buried in a pyramid.

2. True or False: Hatshepsut was a woman pharaoh.

3. True or False: Hieroglyphics is the spoken language of the Egyptians.

4. True or False: The Sphinx was part lion, part woman.

5. True or False: Cleopatra was from Greece.

6. Who was the god of the dead?
    a. Nefertiti   b. Ra   c. Osiris

7. Who was the evil brother of Osiris?
    a. Tutankhamen   b. Set   c. Ramses II

8. What is the name of the stone that broke the hieroglyphics code?
    a. Carlotta   b. Blarney   c. Rosetta

9. All pharaohs wear this animal on their head.
    a. cobra   b. hippopotamus   c. crocodile

10. In what year did Carter discover the tomb of the boy king?
    a. 1492   b. 1776   c. 1922

Answer key to Thoth's questions:

1. False	6. c. Osiris
2. True	7. b. Set
3. False	8. c. Rosetta
4. True	9. a. Cobra
5. True	10. c. 1922

C. Displays

The Persona Pyramid

Take the "Who Am I? work sheets along with the illustrations of the students' personas and create a pyramid on the wall. Simply arrange the work sheets in a triangle on a large wall.

Obelisks

Obelisks are long four-sided towers that are tapered at the top. An example of this large, needlelike structure is the Washington Monument. Most of the obelisks of Egypt were eventually taken to other countries—including France, England, and the United States. During ancient times, hundreds of obelisks lined the banks of the Nile. Ancient Egyptians believed the towers, like the pyramids, possessed great powers. Many obelisks were covered with messages in hieroglyphics.

Use the pattern contained in this unit (see pp. 108 and 109), and have your students create an obelisk. Fold the pattern at the dotted lines. Glue the base together, then cut out the four triangles and glue them together to make the top. Make sure students place a secret message in hieroglyphics on the side.

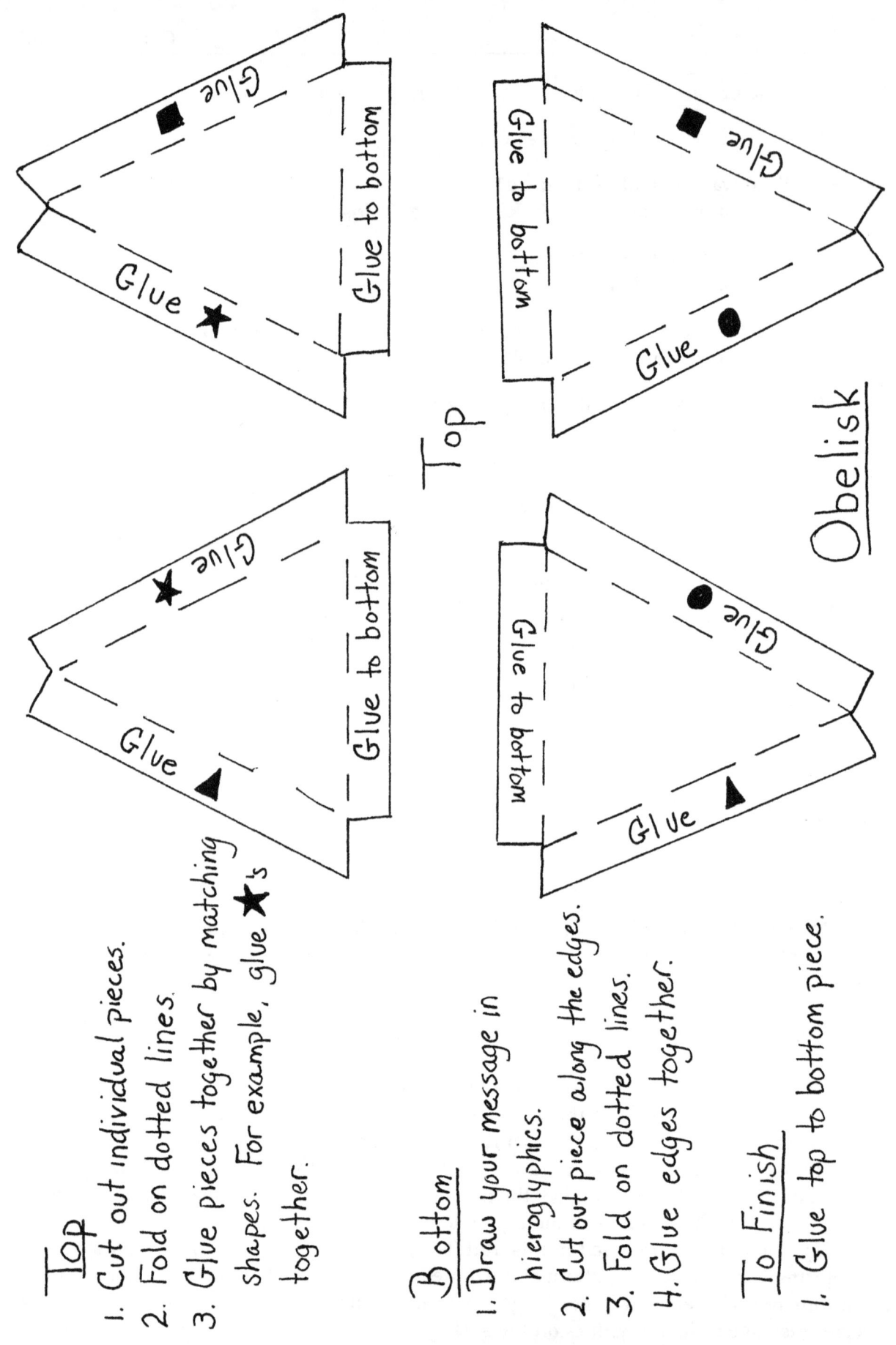

Glue

Bottom Portion of Obelisk

From *The Persona Book.* © 1997. Katherine Lallier and Nancy Marino. TIP. (800) 237-6124.

Rules for Drawing Egyptian Figures

Have you ever wondered why a civilization that created huge pyramids drew human figures in such a stylized manner? Some believe that there were rules, created by Egyptian artists working in the royal court, for drawing the human figure. The purpose was to show every feature of the pharaoh in its best light. This is why the eye is always shown facing the front while the nose is usually profiled. Review with students various Egyptian drawings and figures from books. Have them examine similarities in drawings. Following is a list of rules for drawing Egyptian figures. Place them in a prominent place in the classroom or distribute them to each student. Have students draw their own Egyptian figures.

Eyes face front.

Nose and head are profiled.

Shoulders and chest are full view—facing front.

Elbows, legs, knees, and feet are profiled.

Rosetta Stone and Hieroglyphics

The Rosetta stone, discovered by Jean-François Champollion, solved the mystery of Egyptian hieroglyphics. Create your own Rosetta stone by enlarging the hieroglyphic key in this book. Place it on a large, round tan piece of paper, and display it in a prominent place. Have students decide on their personas' top three characteristics, then code them into hieroglyphics along with their personas' most important deed or contribution. On the back of the paper, students can write the name of their persona—also in hieroglyphics. Place these papers in a box near the Rosetta stone. Students can pick a paper and solve the hieroglyphics. They can try to solve the hieroglyphics on the one side to guess the correct persona.

D. Spectacles

Nothing is more strongly identified with ancient Egyptians than their unequaled skill in the art of mummy making. To the ancient Egyptians, mummification ensured a certain level of immortality. You will not be able to hear a pin drop during the following spectacle.

There should be a solemn, almost ominous tone to this production. The only characters who are mandatory are Osiris and Anubis. Other gods and goddesses may be added or deleted. If you choose to change a particular character, the first sentence needs to be altered to reflect the personality of the new god or goddess.

How to Make an Egyptian Mummy

Characters:

Anubis	*Nephtys*
Chonsu	*Nunu*
Geb	*Osiris*
Hapi	*Ptah*
Hathor	*Sati*
Khnum	*Sebek*
Maat	*A student to perform the "surgery"*

Setting: The setting needs to be dark. There is a large sheet hanging in the center. Behind the sheet is a table on which the body of Osiris rests. A floodlight—we improvised with two overhead projectors—should be directed at Osiris from behind the sheet. This creates a silhouette of the body, which is being prepared for mummification. One student should be behind the sheet with Osiris to perform the "silhouette surgery." He or she needs a long, thin stick with a hook at the end, props representing the organs being removed—spaghetti intestines, a sponge brain, and so on—and gauze or toilet paper to wrap the mummy.

In front of the curtain are the performers. They should be seated on either side of the sheet. Each one holds a percussion instrument: sticks, maracas, a wooden block, a triangle, a tambourine, and so on. As each god prepares to inform the audience about a step in the mummification process, the student should rise, walk to the center of the stage slowly playing his or her instrument, then genuflect to the mummy, turn to the audience, and recite his or her part. Then, while playing the instrument, the student should return to his or her seat.

ANUBIS: I am Anubis, the god of embalming. I have traveled to this world along with other gods of the dead to tell you about ancient Egypt's greatest secret: how to make a mummy. First you must understand that the ancient Egyptians had one great wish, and that was to live forever. Egyptians believed that after they died, a new life began. They would live in their tombs as they had lived on Earth. They would also travel to another world to live with the gods and goddesses of the dead. But for a person's spirit to live forever, it had to be able to recognize and return to its body. If it could not recognize the body from which it arose, it would die. That is why Egyptians preserved the bodies in a lifelike way. Mummification guaranteed the ancient Egyptians their one great wish. My fellow gods and goddesses will share the step-by-step secret of how to make a mummy.

From *The Persona Book.* © 1997. Katherine Lallier and Nancy Marino. TIP. (800) 237-6124.

GEB: I am Geb, the Earth god. The first step in making a mummy was to bathe the body and lay it out on a high table so that the priests and embalmers would not have to bend over.

KHNUM: I am Khnum, the god who created mankind and the lord of the Nile cataracts, or rapids. The next step was to remove the dead man's brain by inserting a long, hooklike instrument into his nose and scooping out the brain in little pieces. Experts did this difficult work, because one wrong move could damage the man's face. Chemicals removed any remaining brain parts.

SATI: I am Sati, the wife of Khnum. It was my pleasure to hunt down and prey on the dead. In the next step, the chief priest painted a line on the left side of the dead body. This line was about five inches long and showed where the abdomen was to be cut open in the next step.

MAAT: I am Maat, the goddess of justice. I weighed the heart of the dead in a special scale to see what kind of person was coming to live among us. In the next step, the priest used a sharp knife called an Ethiopian stone. He cut a hole in the body where the line was. Then he reached in and carefully removed all internal organs. The heart was left in the body because it was the center of knowledge. Taking out the organs was hard work, and the man who did it had to be strong. He was also considered unclean, and others would chase him out of the tent when he was done.

HAPI: I am Hapi, the god who guards the canopic jars. Once the organs were removed, the stomach, liver, lungs, and intestines were mummified separately and placed in special containers called canopic jars. A jar shaped like a man's head held the stomach, and the intestines were put in a jar that was shaped like a dog's head. The lungs were put in a jackal-headed jar, and the liver was placed in a jar with a hawk's head.

SEBEK: They call me Sebek, and I am the crocodile god. In the next step, the torso of the body was now empty, and the embalmers washed it out with palm wine. They rubbed it with perfumes such as myrrh. The wine and

From *The Persona Book.* © 1997. Katherine Lallier and Nancy Marino. TIP. (800) 237-6124.

	perfume not only made the mummy smell good, they were also good preservatives.
CHONSU:	I am Chonsu, the moon god. Now it was time for the padding. The empty torso was stuffed with linen soaked in a natural glue called resin. The padding was used to keep the mummy looking lifelike. For some mummies, this distorted the face.
NUNU:	I am the ocean god, Nunu. In the next step, the body was now ready for drying. It was placed on a special sloped table and covered with natron powder. For two months, the body was dried by chemicals and the sun.
HATHOR:	I am Hathor, protectress of the dead. When the skin was dry and hard as old leather, it was finally time to prepare the mummy for wrapping. The body was bathed and rubbed with spices. The mouth, eyes, and nose were cleaned, stuffed with linen, and sealed with wax. Thin wires of gold were fastened around the fingernails and toenails to keep them from falling off. The embalmers sewed up the hole through which the organs had been removed, and the priests sealed it with a special plate that bore the sacred symbol known as the Eye of Horus. If you look at a dollar bill, you can see what the Eye of Horus looks like.
NEPHTYS:	My name is Nephtys, and I was present at the judging of the heart. Now the mummy was wrapped in the finest linen—between 150 and 350 yards. The wrapping went on for days, and there were many rituals. Some mummies may have been covered with poison to curse the tomb robbers. Amulets and jewelry were placed inside the wrappings to protect the dead on their trip to the underworld. Rings were placed on the fingers, and gold earrings were hung in the person's ears. Finally the wrapped mummy was coated in resin, which hardened like varnish.
PTAH:	I am Ptah, the creator of the universe. While all this was going on, artists were busy making the beautiful coffins that would house the mummy. The dead person's relatives collected food, furniture, and other belongings that his or her spirit would need in the afterlife. After 70 days, it was time for the funeral.

ANUBIS: It is said that the first Egyptian to be mummified was the great king, Osiris. He was embalmed by me, Anubis, the jackal god. When Osiris died he became a god. He was the king of the underworld and prince of the dead. It was to Osiris' kingdom that the dead wished to go.

From *The Persona Book.* © 1997. Katherine Lallier and Nancy Marino. TIP. (800) 237-6124.

Walk Like an Egyptian: A Dance

Another crowd-pleasing spectacle is not based in history or mythology but is a great way to add a festive tone to "Valley of the Kings." Using the Bangles' pop hit, "Walk Like an Egyptian," have your little pharaohs, deities, and archaeologists strut their stuff. The dance need not be complicated if you keep the fabulous choreographer Busby Berkley in mind. Start with a line formation, and have different groups of children do the same steps at different times—first the girls, then the boys or one group of four, then the next group of four and so on. Use all the stereotypical Egyptian hieroglyphic moves. Use some cheerleading maneuvers. Have fun. If the dancers are in costume and the dance has a clean line and is well rehearsed, everyone is bound to have a good time because the song is all in fun.

Bibliography

Aliki. *Mummies Made in Egypt.* New York: HarperCollins, 1979.

Clare, John D. *Pyramids of Ancient Egypt.* San Diego, Calif.: Gulliver Books, 1992.

Climo, Shirley. *The Egyptian Cinderella.* New York: Thomas Y. Crowell, 1989.

Cohen, Daniel. *Ancient Egypt.* New York: Doubleday, 1990.

Crosher, Judith. *Ancient Egypt.* New York: Viking, 1992.

David, Rosalie, and Anthony E. David. *Ancient Egypt.* New York: Warwick Press, 1984.

dePaola, Tomie. *Bill and Pete Go Down the Nile.* New York: G. P. Putnam's Sons, 1987.

Dexter, Catherine. *The Gilded Cat.* New York: William Morrow, 1992.

Eschle, Lou. *The Curse of Tutankhamen.* San Diego, Calif.: Lucent Books, 1994.

Frost, Abigail. *Myths and Legends of Ancient Egypt.* New York: Marshall Cavendish, 1990.

Ganeri, Anita. *Ancient Egyptians.* New York: Shooting Star Press, 1993.

Gerrard, Roy. *Croco'nile.* New York: Farrar, Straus & Giroux, 1994.

Gold, Susan Dudley. *The Pharaoh's Curse.* New York: Crestwood House, 1990.

Hamilton, Virginia. *In the Beginning: Creation Stories Around the World.* San Diego, Calif.: Harcourt Brace Jovanovich, 1988.

Harris, Geraldine. *Gods and Pharaohs from Egyptian Mythology*. New York: Peter Bedrick Books, 1991.

Harris, Nathaniel. *Everyday Life in Ancient Egypt*. New York: Franklin Watts, 1994.

Hart, George. *Eyewitness Books: Ancient Egypt*. New York: Alfred A. Knopf, 1990.

Haslam, Andrew, and Alexandra Parsons. *Make It Work! Ancient Egypt*. London: Thomson Learning, 1995.

Holmes, Burnham. *Nefertiti: The Mystery Queen*. Milwaukee, Wis.: Raintree, 1983.

Karr, Kathleen. *Gideon and the Mummy Professor*. New York: Farrar, Straus & Giroux, 1993.

Koenig, Viviane. *The Ancient Egyptians: Life in the Nile Valley*. Brookfield, Conn.: Millbrook Press, 1992.

Lauber, Patricia. *Tales Mummies Tell*. New York: Thomas Y. Crowell, 1985.

McDermott, Gerald. *The Voyage of Osiris: A Myth of Ancient Egypt*. New York: Windmill Books and E. P. Dutton, 1977.

McDonald, Collin. *Nightwaves: Scary Tales for After Dark*. New York: Cobblehill Books, 1990.

Morley, Jacqueline, et al. *An Egyptian Pyramid*. New York: Peter Bedrick Books, 1991.

Perl, Lila. *Mummies, Tombs, and Treasure: Secrets of Ancient Egypt*. New York: Clarion Books, 1987.

Purdy, Susan, and Cass R. Sandak. *Ancient Egypt: A Civilization Project Book*. New York: Franklin Watts, 1982.

Putnam, James. *Mummy*. Eyewitness Books. New York: Alfred A. Knopf, 1993.

———. *Pyramid*. Eyewitness Books. New York: Alfred A. Knopf, 1994.

Reeves, Nicholas. *Into the Mummy's Tomb: The Real-Life Discovery of Tutankhamen's Treasures*. New York: Scholastic, 1992.

Sabuda, Robert. *Tutankhamen's Gift*. New York: Atheneum, 1994.

Snyder, Zilpha Keatley. *The Egypt Game*. New York: Dell, 1994.

Wilcox, Charlotte. *Mummies and Their Mysteries*. Minneapolis, Minn.: Carolrhoda Books, 1993.

Wright, Rachel. *Egyptians: Facts, Things to Make, Activities*. New York: Franklin Watts, 1992.

Software

Annabel's Dream of Ancient Egypt. CD-ROM. Texas Caviar Inc., Austin, Tex.

Crossword & Wordgames. CD-ROM for IBM. Expert Software Inc., Coral Gables, Fla.

Nile Passage to Egypt. CD-ROM. Windows/Macintosh. Discovery Channel Multimedia, Bethesda, Md.

4 Voices of the Civil War

Understanding the Civil War Through a Variety of Sources, Including Historical Fiction and Biography

Table of Contents

Voices of the Civil War Personas List	118
Step One: Prepersona Activities	122
Step Two: Decision Making	123
Step Three: Discovery Period	126
Culminating Activities	129
A. Dramas	129
B. Activities And Games	138
C. Displays	147
D. Spectacles	149
Bibliography	154

Voices of the Civil War

For four years, the Civil War raged throughout the United States. Political ideals and basic human rights were at stake. It is, perhaps, the most pivotal event that has shaped our country. The price was high: More American lives were lost in the War Between the States than in any war before or since, and we suffered the loss of one of our greatest presidents by assassination.

The war had many points of view. Both Northern and Southern white men fought for their beliefs, but they were, at times, forced to kill friends and family. Black men who had lived under the tyranny of slavery had to fight for the right to take up arms in pursuit of their personal cause. Women found their roles as wives and mothers expanded to include nursing, spying, and disguising themselves as soldiers. Even children had a part in such great battles as Shiloh and Gettysburg.

The great American poet Walt Whitman said, "The real war will never get in books." The real war was about individuals struggling through the hardships and perils of battle. The Civil War included many individuals, each with his or her own voice. There were the great generals, such as Ulysses S. Grant and Robert E. Lee; politicians, such as Abraham Lincoln and Jefferson Davis; and the healers, including Clara Barton and Dorothea Dix. There were the lesser-known voices of the black soldiers, such as Robert Smalls and William Carney; women soldiers, including Sarah Edmonds and Loreta Velazquez; and clandestine spies, such as Elizabeth Van Lew and Rose O'Neal Greenhow. Finally, there was the commitment of the abolitionists—from John Brown to Harriet Tubman to the author of *Uncle Tom's Cabin*, Harriet Beecher Stowe. Each contributed his or her own point of view to the Civil War era.

The following unit seeks to discover the faces behind the dates of this tragic American event. Using the actual historical personalities, students will develop a personal "voice" for the people who shaped the Civil War.

Do not attempt all of the activities. Choose only those that suit your style of teaching or your students' particular learning needs. Perhaps for the first time, try the *tableaux-vivants* and the Civil War memorial. Save the dramas and the battle for the following year. Any of these activities will allow your students to experience the War Between the States in a more personal way.

Voices of the Civil War Persona List

The purpose of the persona list is to easily identify significant people in the Civil War. It is in no way inclusive of all the brave men and women who were involved in this conflict. It represents famous, infamous, and barely known players who characterized differing points of view or "voices." There are nine "regiments" represented in this unit with room for others of your own design. Other personalities can be added or deleted from any of the groups. The persona sketches are brief and should only act as a reminder for students and teachers involved in the project. Because students create their own persona description, this list should only be used as a referral. More detailed descriptions should come from the children who choose them. This list will be used in conjunction with the decision-making lesson after children have become acquainted with several of the historical personas.

Voices of the Civil War Persona List 119

The Civil War personas are divided into "regiments." Each regiment consists of people who share a similar goal and collective voice. The regiments are Voices of the South, Union Voices, Voices of the Black Soldiers, Voices of the Women Soldiers, Rebel Voices, Abolitionist Voices, Red Cross Voices, the Presidents' Voices, and a Voice with a Picture.

By acquainting themselves with these regiments, students can learn about the Civil War from a multicultural point of view. Short biographies of most of these personas can be found in *An American Civil War: A Multicultural Encyclopedia*.

Voices of the South

This group reflects the views of the "old South" that were popular during the antebellum period, which included the years 1820 to 1860.

Belle Boyd: The South's most famous spy.

Letitia Burwell: A Southern belle who believed slaves were happy and carefree.

Mary Chestnut: Famous for her diaries.

Jefferson Davis: The Confederacy's first and only president.

Rose O'Neal Greenhow: A spy for the South who lived in Washington, D.C.

James "Jeb" Ewell Brown Stuart: Confederate cavalry leader.

Union Voices

This group is represented by some of the greatest military leaders fighting for the preservation of the Union. There are individual biographies for many of these men, but look to Civil War books on their individual battles and engagements for more information.

Major Robert Anderson: The commanding officer at Fort Sumter.

Rear Admiral D. G. Farragut: First admiral in the United States.

Ulysses Simpson Grant: The last of Lincoln's chief generals.

Winfield Scott Hancock: An honest and intelligent leader.

George McClellan: General who hesitated in battle.

General Irvin McDowell: General defeated at Bull Run.

General Winfield Scott: A 70-year-old general who was the first to suggest a Confederate blockade.

General Philip Sheridan: Known for his temper and his skilled horsemanship.

William Tecumseh Sherman: A ruthless general.

Voices of the Black Soldiers

With the exception of Robert Smalls, little is known about individual black soldiers. However, their role was so significant that it even inspired the making of the major motion picture *Glory*. Their stories can be found in such books as Mettger's *Till Victory Is Won: Black Soldiers in the Civil War*; and Reef's *Civil War Soldiers*.

William Carney: A member of the all-black 54th Massachusetts Regiment.

Lewis H. Douglass: Fought with the 54th Massachusetts Regiment.

Christian Fleetwood: Received the U.S. Medal of Honor for extreme valor.

Robert Smalls: Escaped slave and Union Navy captain.

Voices of the Women Soldiers

With the exception of Sarah Edmonds, little is known about the women who disguised themselves as soldiers. No one knows for sure, but it is thought that hundreds of women disguised themselves to serve on the front lines. Their unique position in the war can be found in Chang's *A Separate Battle: Women and the Civil War*; Colman's *Spies! Women in the Civil War*; and Canon's *Civil War Heroines*.

Kady Brownell: She fought alongside her husband for the Union.

Amy Clark: She continued to fight in the war even after her Confederate husband was killed.

Sarah Edmonds: She disguised herself as a man and became a nurse for the Union.

Jennie Hodgers: She fought for the Union under the name Albert Cashier.

Loreta Velazquez: To fight for the South, she disguised herself as a man.

Rebel Voices

This group represents some of the greatest military leaders who fought for the Confederacy. There are individual biographies on many of these men, but look to specific battles and engagements for more information.

General Pierre Beauregard: The hot-tempered general who fired on Fort Sumter.

Braxton Bragg: Violent-tempered and disliked general.

Jubal Anderson Early: Feisty, unkempt, and one of the South's favorite generals.

Thomas J. "Stonewall" Jackson: Lee's most trusted general.

Robert E. Lee: Considered one of the greatest military men in history.

James Longstreet: "Old Pete" was a tough rebel general.

George E. Pickett: Known for his ill-fated charge at Gettysburg.

Abolitionist Voices

This regiment is perhaps the most eclectic. Through various methods and a variety of reasons, these men and women fought the "peculiar institution" of slavery in their own way. Look for individual biographies on many of these people as well as books on the Underground Railroad.

Mary Elizabeth Bowser: Freed slave who became a spy for the Union forces.

John Brown: Militant abolitionist hanged at Harpers Ferry.

Frederick Douglass: Former slave known for his eloquent antislavery speeches.

Charlotte Forten: A young, free African American woman who taught contraband children.

Angelina Grimke: A Charleston belle appalled at how slaves were treated.

Harriet Beecher Stowe: Author of *Uncle Tom's Cabin* in 1852.

Sojourner Truth: A deeply religious abolitionist, feminist, and escaped slave.

Harriet Tubman: The Underground Railroad's most famous conductor.

Elizabeth Van Lew: "Crazy Betsy" was a famous Union spy.

Red Cross Voices

The professionalism that women such as Clara Barton and Dorothea Dix offered the world of nursing changed the job description forever. Other women who volunteered discovered the agony of war through horrific hospital conditions. Chang's *A Separate Battle: Women and the Civil War* is one source for learning about these heroines of the war.

Louisa May Alcott: Author and volunteer nurse for the Yankees.

Clara Barton: Founded the Red Cross in the United States in 1881 after doing nursing work throughout the Civil War.

Mary Ann Bickerdyke: A tough Union nurse.

Kate Cumming: A Confederate nurse who was present at the Battle of Shiloh.

Dorothea Dix: "Dragon Dix" was a Union nurse who improved conditions for the mentally ill.

Mary Livermore: She raised much money for Civil War Union soldiers.

The Presidents' Voices

This country's 15th, 16th, and 17th presidents all had to deal with the issues of secession, slavery, and emancipation. Read individual biographies for their differing views and motives.

John Wilkes Booth: Shot Lincoln at point-blank range.

James Buchanan: The Union began to fall apart while he was in office.

Andrew Johnson: Succeeded Lincoln as 17th president.

Abraham Lincoln: President during the Civil War.

A Voice with a Picture

This trio had a different perspective of the war from anyone else. Two chronicled it through images saved for posterity. One desperately tried to escape its effects only to be trapped in its web.

Mathew B. Brady: The war's best-known photographer.

Wilmer McLean: The war began in his yard and ended in his front parlor.

Alfred R. Waud: The artist who sketched battles, including the fighting at Gettysburg.

Step One: Prepersona Activities

1. Read several short works of fiction to introduce children to the Civil War. Some great books to read aloud are Gauch's *Thunder at Gettysburg,* Josephs's *Mountain Boy,* and Polacco's *Pink and Say.* Reading about slavery and the Underground Railroad is another important dimension when studying the Civil War. Ringgold's *Aunt Harriet's Underground Railroad in the Sky* is a unique picture-book fantasy about Harriet Tubman. Rappaport's *Escape from Slavery: Five Journeys to Freedom* includes a tale that is reminiscent of Harriet Beecher Stowe's *Uncle Tom's Cabin,* the book that ignited the North and South.

2. Persona-based enrichment provides many avenues for learning about the War Between the States. You will, however, want to provide some background. Start by introducing the political climate directly before the Civil War. Topics that may be covered are slavery, the Underground Railroad, the antebellum South, Southern versus Northern industry, and Lincoln's bumpy road to the White House. These topics are also explored in the persona-based projects.

3. Develop a strategy to introduce children to role playing: Read Gauch's *Thunder at Gettysburg* aloud to your class. To encourage children to start thinking in the first person, ask them the following questions. Their responses may be written or oral.
    What if you were Tillie? When you were safe in your parents' house before the battle, what did you expect to see? Was it different from what you saw? Why would you "never want to forget" that week in July?
    Another book that can be used to introduce students to role playing is *Mountain Boy.* Written by nine-year-old Anna Catherine Josephs, this book tells how her great-grandfather helped soldiers who escaped from a Confederate prison find freedom in Tennessee. After reading the story, encourage students to start role-playing by asking them the following questions:

A. In the beginning of the story, the author explains that some of Tommy's brothers were fighting on the side of the North and others were fighting on the side of the South. What if you were Tommy and had brothers fighting on both sides of the war? How would you feel about the war?

B. If you were Tommy, how would you feel during your 52-day journey? What would keep you from leaving the prisoners, turning around, and going home?

C. What if you were the escaped prisoners? How would you feel if you were following a young boy to safety?

D. What if you were Tommy's mother? Would you let him go on the journey?

Step Two: Decision Making

After students are familiar with some of the historical figures of the Civil War, the persona element can be introduced.

1. Explain to students that they will be choosing a persona and doing projects as that persona. Talk about some of the culminating projects. Explain as well that for this unit they will be working in "regiments." They will work on some projects individually; on others they will work with their regiments. Each regiment consists of people who share a similar goal or collective voice. The regiments are Voices of the South, Union Voices, Voices of the Black Soldiers, Voices of the Women Soldiers, Rebel Voices, Abolitionist Voices, Red Cross Voices, Presidents' Voices, and a Voice with a Picture.

2. Each student will be asked to make three choices of possible personas. They will be asked to give reasons why they chose a particular regiment or a certain character. These reasons will be important if two or more children want to be the same persona.

3. Place a copy of the "Voices of the Civil War" criteria for decision making in a visible place, and give each student a copy of the criteria. Encourage children to invent additional criteria. See the next page for a copy of the decision-making form.

4. Review the different regiments and the personas included in each group. Allow students to refer to the list of personas when making their choices.

5. Explain that in addition to specific personas, a student can opt to create a persona for a regiment. For example, if a student wishes to become an abolitionist, a soldier, or a slave, the student must create a name and a personal history.

6. Ask the students to complete the "Voices of the Civil War" decision-making work sheet.

7. For the lesson that follows, have a conference with each student. It is especially important to talk with students who did not get their first choice, because all should be happy with their choices.

Name _____

VOICES OF THE CIVIL WAR
DECISION-MAKING WORK SHEET

DECISION: WHICH REGIMENT WILL I CHOOSE FOR MY CIVIL WAR VOICE?

ALTERNATIVES:

Voices of the South *Abolitionist Voices*
Union Voices *Red Cross Voices*
Voices of the Black Soldiers *The Presidents' Voices*
Voices of the Women Soldiers *The Voice with a Picture*
Rebel Voices

DECISION:

Answer the questions on the following page. Use your answers to make a decision, and give reasons for your decision. The more thorough your answer, the more likely it is that you will receive your choice. List two alternatives.

Give three choices in order of preference.

1. _____

2. _____

3. _____

From *The Persona Book.* © 1997. Katherine Lallier and Nancy Marino. TIP. (800) 237-6124.

Name _____

VOICES OF THE CIVIL WAR
DECISION-MAKING WORK SHEET

Page 2

DECISION: WHICH REGIMENT WILL I CHOOSE FOR MY CIVIL WAR VOICE?

1. Am I interested in this point of view?

2. Will I enjoy exploring the lives of the people in this regiment?

3. Will I do extra research concerning this character?

4. Will I be able to design and make a costume for this persona?

5. Is there a particular persona in this regiment that I would like to portray?

From *The Persona Book*. © 1997. Katherine Lallier and Nancy Marino. TIP. (800) 237-6124.

Step Three: Discovery Period

One way to familiarize students with the Civil War is simply to immerse them in the topic. Dedicate a day—at the very least a morning—to exploration. Set up a readathon in the library or your classroom for the purpose of gathering knowledge about the war. To foster the students' enjoyment of this discovery period, encourage them to bring in sleeping bags and snacks. Consider setting up a tent or tents to give the feel of a Civil War military camp.

To begin your readathon, start with a selection you can read aloud to your students. Polacco's picture book *Pink and Say* is an excellent choice. This beautifully illustrated book tells the true story of a black and a white Union soldier. Neither is more than 15 years old. The black boy, "Pink," rescues "Say," who has been wounded and takes him home to his grandmother. There, Pink teaches his white friend how to read, and the two discuss their feelings about the war while Say recovers from his wounds. In the end, they are caught by Confederates. Say is sent to Andersonville Prison, but Pink is immediately hanged because of the color of his skin. Say survives the war and vows that all his family for generations to come will remember Pink because he has no family of his own to do it for him.

After everyone has listened to this story, you may wish to have a brief discussion about the book. Your students might create a list of everything they already know about the Civil War and a list of things they would like to discover.

Next, saturate students with every book, computer program, and resource available on the war. Lay the materials out so that they are readily available. To give focus to the immersion process, have children work in pairs or small groups while participating in this chapter's scavenger hunt. Review the hunt, however, to ensure that your students can find the answers in your resources. Most of the questions are general and should be easily available—with the exception of the names of famous generals' horses. These names can be found, however, in Boatner's *The Civil War Dictionary* as well as in other resources listed in the bibliography.

Once children start their research for the scavenger hunt, they are usually enthralled with the point system that allows them to be promoted through the ranks by correct answers. See the end of the scavenger hunt for details on how children "win."

The readathon-scavenger hunt is a fun-filled, exciting way to expose students to such a vast topic. Fiction and nonfiction video shorts—included in the bibliography—can be shown to break up the day. At the end of the day, you may wish to have students select a Civil War historical fiction to read during the unit, but keep these books in a separate area until the scavenger hunt is over.

Students can create persona journals. Every time they learn about a new event or battle, students can write about it in their journal. These journals, written in the first person, can include answers to questions.

Describe your personality.

    What was my physical appearance?

    What did I wear?

    What dangers did I face?

    What was my position in the war?

Letters from the Front

Another variation on a journal is a "letter from the front." The student can write letters from their persona to another persona in the classroom. It can be about a particular event or describe the hardships of war.

Surf the Net

Many Americans have a great interest in studying the Civil War. Their curiosity is reflected in the number of sites available on the Internet. Below is a sample:

The Civil War Center

> http://www.cwc.lsu.edu/civlink.htm

The Civil War Center provides access to a multitude of Civil War sites and information about the period. Flags of the Civil War, diaries of soldiers, and a list of historic places are all found here.

Abraham Lincoln Online

> http://www.netins.net/showcase/creative/lincoln.html

This site includes a section called "This Week in Lincoln History" as well as Lincoln's speeches and writing.

Selected Civil War Pictures

> http://lcweb.loc.gov/spcoll/048.html

This Library of Congress site contains more than 1,000 photographs of the Civil War. Many of these pictures found on the World Wide Web page were made under the supervision of Mathew Brady.

Who Am I?

The "Who Am I?" work sheet (see page 128), encourages children to create a legacy for their tombstones (see "Civil War Memorial" for more information). This writing task is one of the important culminating activities but is also one of the most difficult tasks. To ease the student into the writing process, the following questionnaire is provided. The results, written in the first person, will be included as part of the "Civil War Memorial." Students may also design a picture of their persona to accompany the creative writing.

Student's Name _____

Persona's Name _____

VOICES OF THE CIVIL WAR
WHO AM I? WORK SHEET

Whether your persona is a Southern general, an abolitionist, or a soldier, you must let everyone know who you are. In no fewer than six sentences, tell about yourself. Be sure to include some of the information from your journals.

Examples of what you might include are:

1. What is your job or purpose?

2. What is your position in the Civil War?

3. Tell a story about yourself or tell of an accomplishment.

4. How are you alike and how are you different from the others in your regiment?

5. What kind of dangers or hardships do you face?

6. How would you describe yourself? Some choices: brave, ruthless, wild, heroic, fearless, afraid, curious, obedient, confident, smart, dedicated, loyal, humble, evil, honest, sly, fair.

From *The Persona Book*. © 1997. Katherine Lallier and Nancy Marino. TIP. (800) 237-6124.

Readers' Theater

An excellent way to introduce your students to the Civil War through literature is to use Fleischman's *Bull Run*. The author creates 16 distinct, fictional voices—only Irvin McDowell's story is factual—to describe the feelings and experiences of the people who were touched by the Civil War's first major battle. Each chapter in the book is told by a different character—though all the narrators recur in other stories. This novel is a wonderful book to read aloud but was really meant to be used as a readers' theater.

A form of creative dramatization and oral expression, readers' theater allows each participant to read his or her part aloud. Readers must review their lines a number of times to present their ideas dramatically. But the words are never memorized because the focus is on reading.

Fleischman wrote the stories with readers' theater in mind. At the end of the book, he lists the characters and page numbers so that a class might perform the work. *Bull Run* not only introduces this important battle, it clarifies the idea of a persona.

Culminating Activities

There are many interesting activities in store for your regiments in "Voices of the Civil War." The following events allow your students to share their personas' stories with everyone. "Voices of the Civil War" is a collection of displays, demonstrations, and interactive happenings that center on this historical American event that defined us as a nation.

Below are the types of culminating activities for this unit. Select as many activities as you will need for all your students to participate.

Dramas: If your students love the idea of putting on a play, choose some of the skits included in this chapter. Students should be encouraged to enhance and elaborate on the dramas provided or, better yet, to create their own.

Activities and Games: Use activities if you want the entire school or just selected grade levels to participate in "Voices of the Civil War." The personas who are listed for these activities should organize and manage the events with the teacher taking on the role of adviser.

Displays: These art projects are the perfect way to transform your classroom, library, or auditorium into a battlefield.

Spectacles: The activities can be performed in front of a large audience. They are usually favorites with participants and spectators alike.

A. Dramas

On October 12, 1870, General Robert E. Lee, commander of the Army of Northern Virginia and the South's greatest hero, died of natural causes in his home. It is said that before he died, Lee's mind drifted back to wartime. The following script is a fictionalized account of what the general may have been thinking in the hours before his death. Your students can use this script or write their own based on what they think Lee was dreaming.

A FINAL FAREWELL
THE DEATH OF ROBERT E. LEE

Characters:
Clara Barton
Jefferson Davis
Ulysses S. Grant
Thomas "Stonewall" Jackson
Robert E. Lee
Abraham Lincoln
Narrator: Wilmer McLean

Setting: The deathbed of General Lee. He is visited by Civil War memories on October 11, 1870, the evening before his death.

WILMER McLEAN: Only five years ago, America was involved in a terrible war. Some people called it the Civil War, while others called it the War Between the States. No matter. By 1865, more than 600,000 Americans were dead. In my book, that means nobody wins. The Southern general Robert E. Lee surrendered to the Northern general Ulysses S. Grant at Appomattox Courthouse—my front parlor! That's a funny coincidence, considering the whole blasted thing started in my yard at Bull Run. No matter. The war is over now. Although the great Robert E. Lee survived the war, he is now about ready to die. His mind keeps drifting back to the war. Take a look. . . .

ROBERT E. LEE: Mary, Mary, are you there? I'm not feeling well. I need some water. Traveller needs some water too. You must treat your horse with great respect, you know. Oh, Traveller, you were my closest companion. We saw it all together—triumph and tragedy. I'll always wonder, though, did I do the right thing?

ABRAHAM LINCOLN: General Lee.

LEE: Mary, is it you?

LINCOLN: No, General, it is your president. It is Abraham Lincoln who stands before you. *(Lee tries to rise.)* Don't try to get up. I can see you're not well.

LEE: Mr. President, what can I do for you?

LINCOLN: There's a great rebellion brewing in the South, General. I need someone strong and reliable to command the Union forces. Can I depend on you?

From The Persona Book. © 1997. Katherine Lallier and Nancy Marino. TIP. (800) 237-6124.

LEE:	I've heard that there is talk of seceding from the Union because of the slavery issue.
LINCOLN:	Where do you stand on the issue of secession and slavery, General?
LEE:	I hate both ideas. Slavery is a horrid institution, and secession from the United States is unthinkable.
LINCOLN:	Then we think alike. You stand with me.
LEE:	We do think alike, Mr. President, but I am a Virginian. I must stand with my state even if I don't agree with her. Virginia is my home. I'm sorry, Mr. Lincoln, I must resign my commission in the United States Army.
LINCOLN:	Do you know what you're doing, General?

(Enter Davis)

JEFFERSON DAVIS:	Of course he does. He shall become the leader of the Confederate forces and keep you Yankees out of our affairs. Mr. Lincoln, you are no longer welcome here.
LINCOLN:	Good-bye, General, I shall sorely miss your talent on the battlefield. *(He exits)*
LEE:	Mr. Lincoln, are you still here?
DAVIS:	No, Robert. I told that Yankee to leave. It's your new president, Jefferson Davis, who stands before you now.
LEE:	Mr. Davis…
DAVIS:	I'm glad you told that Yankee scoundrel you were part of the Confederate States of America now.
LEE:	I told Mr. Lincoln I was a Virginian first…
DAVIS:	Yes, and Virginia has joined the rest of the South in our noble cause. States' rights must come first. Each state must make its own rules to live by. We will not have the North dictate our lives, Robert!
LEE:	I don't think that is what Mr. Lincoln wants either.

DAVIS:	I don't care what Mr. Lincoln wants! He wants you to fight on the Union side, but he can't have you! You will lead the Army of Northern Virginia against Lincoln and the rest of those Yankees or die in the attempt! Good day, General Lee!
LEE:	Good day, Mr. Davis. (*Davis exits*)
THOMAS "STONEWALL" JACKSON:	Ain't he a piece of work, General?
LEE:	Thomas, is that you? I've missed you, Stonewall.
JACKSON:	We were quite a team, eh? Robert E. Lee and Stonewall Jackson—the unbeatable. Our battle at Chancellorsville was remarkable, if I do say so myself. It was probably our single greatest moment of glory.
LEE:	And my greatest defeat. After all, I lost you, Thomas, my most trusted friend.
JACKSON:	You did me proud, Robert. You did the South proud.
LEE:	But at what cost? Perhaps I was too good at what I did. Maybe it would have been better if the war had been lost sooner. We never stood a chance. . . .
JACKSON:	General, you allowed Southerners to keep their dignity, and that is worth everything.
CLARA BARTON:	Pardon me, but are you General Lee? (*Exit Jackson*) I need to speak to you and General Grant about those poor boys fighting each other.
LEE:	How can I help you, madam?
BARTON:	My name is Clara Barton, General Lee. I have been nursing the wounded—mostly in the North. I know my Southern sisters feel the same about the horrible conditions in treating the fallen soldiers.
LEE:	The casualties of war weigh heavy on my heart, madam.
BARTON:	Do they, sir? If they did, I do not believe men could wage such terrible cruelty on one another. This war is literally brother against brother. Those who are wounded are far worse off than those who are killed. Young boys are

From *The Persona Book*. © 1997. Katherine Lallier and Nancy Marino. TIP. (800) 237-6124.

	having their arms and legs cut off without any medicine to kill the pain! Hospital conditions are shameful! I assure you, General Lee, there is nothing glorious about war!
LEE:	I assure you, Mrs. Barton, I know. There is nothing glorious about war. . . .

(Exit Barton.)

ULYSSES S. GRANT:	Don't beat yourself up about it, Lee. You did your duty, as I did mine.
LEE:	General Grant?
GRANT:	Yes, Robert. It's me. Old Unconditional Surrender himself.
LEE:	You were my greatest foe, Grant. I truly feared your nickname Unconditional Surrender until our fateful meeting at Appomattox Courthouse. But you were more than fair in regard to the terms of surrender. You sent my troops home with their self-respect. For that I will always be grateful.
GRANT:	It is as much as you would have done for my men. You were a magnificent general but an even greater man. It was my privilege to meet you on the field of battle as well as the field of honor. You followed your heart and your conscience. That is all anyone can ask of himself.
LEE:	Thank you, General Grant. Your words will help my soul rest.
GRANT:	Rest in peace, you old gray fox. Rest in peace. *(Exit Grant)*
LEE:	Strike the tent. *(Lee dies)*
McLEAN:	On the morning of October 12, 1870, Robert E. Lee died. His last words, *Strike the tent*, instructed his men to break down the camp. After the Civil War, Lee had urged his fellow Southerners to accept peace and put the war behind them. But for Robert E. Lee the war weighed heavy on his heart to his dying day.

From *The Persona Book*. © 1997. Katherine Lallier and Nancy Marino. TIP. (800) 237-6124.

Ready for Battle

The next performance imagines all the Union generals and all the Southern generals sitting around discussing the possibility of an upcoming war. Students are encouraged to add to this script or to create their own script. Not only does it examine the personalities of the generals, it also details the strengths and weaknesses of both sides.

Characters:

North
- *Major Robert Anderson*
- *Rear Admiral D. G. Farragut*
- *General Ulysses S. Grant*
- *General Winfield Scott Hancock*
- *General George McClellan*
- *General Winfield Scott*
- *General William Tecumseh Sherman*

South
- *General Pierre Beauregard*
- *General Braxton Bragg*
- *General Jubal Anderson Early*
- *General Thomas J. "Stonewall" Jackson*
- *General Robert E. Lee*
- *General James Longstreet*
- *General George E. Pickett*

Setting: There are two tables. They are supposed to be in two different rooms, but they are on the stage simultaneously. The Southern generals are seated at one table and the Union generals at the other. There are two conversations going on at once. Each group is unaware of the other's discussion.

GENERAL JAMES LONGSTREET: Gentleman, it looks like we're going to have a war.

MAJOR ROBERT ANDERSON: The South wants to secede. They want to leave the Union.

GENERAL WINFIELD SCOTT HANCOCK: They insist on having slaves. They will fight to keep men locked up in chains.

GENERAL PIERRE BEAUREGARD: Well, if it's war they want, then I, General Pierre Beauregard, will fight for the land I love.

GENERAL BRAXTON BRAGG: If those Yankees try to take our land, we'll smash them to pieces. We'll take them down. They'll be whistling "Dixie" before I'm through with them.

GENERAL JUBAL ANDERSON EARLY: You've got quite a temper there, Braxton Bragg. If we're going to fight, we need a strategy.

From *The Persona Book.* © 1997. Katherine Lallier and Nancy Marino. TIP. (800) 237-6124.

REAR ADMIRAL D. G. FARRAGUT:	Anyone have any ideas on how we are going to put an end to this Southern rebellion?
GENERAL WINFIELD SCOTT:	I have a plan. If it is going to work, then it needs your navy expertise, Admiral Farragut. I think we should create a blockade to all the Southern ports.
FARRAGUT:	You mean keep the Southern ships from sailing through, and stop them from trading with Europe? If they can't trade, they are in trouble. They need to trade to buy weapons. They don't manufacture weapons in the South.
SCOTT:	Exactly. And there's another thing. We have to control the Mississippi River. If we do, we can cut off Louisiana, Texas, and Arkansas from the rest of the Confederacy. We've got to keep that cotton from leaving the country. If we do, the war will be over in two or three years.

(The other generals laugh.)

GENERAL WILLIAM TECUMSEH SHERMAN:	Two or three years? Why this rebellion will be over in two or three months. And they say *I'm* the one who's "gone in the head."
SCOTT:	This old body may not work so good, but there is certainly nothing wrong with my mind.
GENERAL GEORGE E. PICKETT:	So, General Jackson, what if the North attacks? Do we have a plan?
GENERAL THOMAS "STONEWALL" JACKSON:	Let them attack us. We will fight on our ground, on our land. We know all the roads, every little footpath, every swamp. We are closer to our food and other suppliers. They come from far away, which means their supplies are farther away.
GENERAL GEORGE McCLELLAN:	We don't even have maps of the South. We are fighting on unfamiliar territory.

From *The Persona Book*. © 1997. Katherine Lallier and Nancy Marino. TIP. (800) 237-6124.

ANDERSON:	Our armed forces are disorganized. We will have to get them into shape.
LONGSTREET:	We don't even have an army, a government, or a constitution. We need someone to put this all together. We have to fight as a united South.
BRAGG:	My friend Jefferson Davis will get all that straightened out. You can be sure of that.
PICKETT:	One thing I know for sure, we have the best military generals in the world sitting here in this room. There's none finer. *(The others nod.)*
GENERAL ULYSSES S. GRANT:	Robert E. Lee is a great general. He's brave and intelligent, and he will fight hard for the Southern cause. Still, we have a working government. That's more than the South has. We have a state department, a postal service, the White House, and a judicial system. The South has to start a government. We've had one here for 75 years.

General Robert E. Lee [Joey Gallagher.]

HANCOCK:	We also have railroads to transport supplies. The South doesn't have that either.
BEAUREGARD:	We have a right to have slaves. It's important to our economy. It's our right to secede from this tyrannical government. What do you think, General Lee?
GENERAL ROBERT E. LEE:	I don't believe in slavery, and *secession* is another word for revolution.
BRAGG:	(*Angrily*) Does that mean you are not going to fight with us, General Lee?
LEE:	My loyalties lie with Virginia. I cannot raise my hand against my birthplace, my home, and my children.
SHERMAN:	They are nothing but a nation of farmers. With all their men fighting in the war, there will be no one to farm their land. They are bound to fail.
HANCOCK:	We will win! Victory is ours!
FARRAGUT:	Damn the torpedoes. Full steam ahead!
LONGSTREET:	We have leadership on our side. The wealthy farmers could become captains and colonels of their units, and the others could take their place alongside them.
PICKETT:	Seventy-five years ago, we defeated the British. We took on the greatest army in the world then. We can do it now.
JACKSON:	We have strength! We Southerners will defend our homeland. Victory is ours!

(*A drum role starts in the background. All of the performers get up and line up, side by side, facing the audience.*)

McCLELLAN:	The war lasted longer than even General Winfield Scott predicted. It was the bloodiest war in the history of the United States. Each of the generals on this stage played a major role in history. Some fought bravely. Some fought so poorly they were relieved of their posts. Some emerged heroes, and others lost their lives.

(Each general steps forward and salutes. If you wish as they salute, they can say a line or two about their role in the Civil War. See the following example.)

BEAUREGARD: I, General Pierre Beauregard, led my troops to victory at Fort Sumter and the Battle of Bull Run.

ANDERSON: I, Major Robert Anderson, was the commanding officer at Fort Sumter. I refused to surrender to the Confederate troops even though there were only 68 Union soldiers inside the fort.

(After they have finished, the generals march off the stage.)

From *The Persona Book.* © 1997. Katherine Lallier and Nancy Marino. TIP. (800) 237-6124.

B. Activities and Games

Tableaux-Vivants, or "Living Pictures"

This was a popular parlor game in the 1800s. In the game's original form, a group of people would decide on a scene—historical or literary. They would then pose as people in that scene, or "tableau." They would neither speak nor act, and others would have to guess the scene.

A variation of this activity can be used for the Civil War personas. Each "regiment" gets together and chooses a painting that represents their collective voice. For example, the abolitionists might choose a picture of a slave mother being separated from her child. The students then enlarge this picture on a large mural and dress in the character of their personas. They then stand in front of their mural to create a "tableau," or living picture. When onlookers go up to the picture, they can ask a question, which the living picture can answer. Post sample questions near each mural to encourage your audience to ask questions. Following are sample questions for each "regiment":

Red Cross Voices

What were hospital conditions like during the war?

What sort of education did you need to become a nurse?

Abolitionist Voices

What methods were used by abolitionists to end slavery?

What was the Underground Railroad?

Voices of the Women Soldiers

Why did you choose to dress up like a man and go into battle?

How were you able to conceal your identity for many months?

Voices of the Black Soldiers

How were you treated differently from white Union soldiers?

What was the 54th Massachusetts Regiment?

Voices of the South

Why did you want to secede from the Union?

What purpose did slavery serve in the South?

Union Voices

What was your army's greatest strength? What advantage did your army have over the South?

What was your army's greatest victory?

Rebel Voices

What was your army's greatest strength? What advantage did your army have over the North?

What was your army's greatest victory?

Voices with a Picture

What does the saying "A picture is worth a thousand words" mean to you?

What impact did you have on the war?

The Lincoln-Douglas Debates

In 1858, Abraham Lincoln, a Republican, was making a bid for the Illinois State Senate. He challenged Democrat Stephen Douglas to a series of debates. Although Lincoln lost the election, he made his mark in the debates by setting forth the differences over slavery. In one of the seven meetings between the two, Lincoln is famous for saying, "A house divided against itself cannot stand." Abraham Lincoln inspired the nation as an orator and was elected president of the United States in 1860.

Using the Lincoln-Douglas debates as a springboard, introduce your students to the basic tenets of debating. An essential element to this oral art is the ability to argue for ideas one may be opposed to personally. It asks students to research their topic thoroughly so that they will be prepared for the opposition. They must then present their ideas in an orderly, logical, and persuasive manner. They learn how to express their opinions and respect the opinions of others, and they gain the ability to think on their feet.

Text continues on page 144.

Team Members' Names: _____

THE CIVIL WAR SCAVENGER HUNT

1. Can you list the states that seceded from the Union?

2. Name any 10 states or territories that fought for the Union. (There are 23 including border states.)

3. Who was president before Abraham Lincoln?

4. Find two Harriets.

5. Who wrote an antislavery book Uncle Tom's Cabin?

6. Who was the Confederate president?

7. Find three abolitionists.

8. Who was hanged at Harpers Ferry?

9. The capture of what fort began the Civil War?

10. How many battles of Bull Run were there?

11. Name the famous ironclad warships for the North and for the South. (Hint: they both begin with m.)

12. The Battle of Antietam was the single bloodiest day of fighting. What was the date?

From *The Persona Book*. © 1997. Katherine Lallier and Nancy Marino. TIP. (800) 237-6124.

Team Members' Names: _____

THE CIVIL WAR SCAVENGER HUNT
(continued)

13. *Here's a tough one, but right under your nose. Ulysses S. Grant had a nickname to match his first two initials. Can you find it?*

14. *Speaking of nicknames, where did Stonewall Jackson get his?*

15. *Write the first six words of the Gettysburg Address.*

16. *Geography time: In which state is Gettysburg?*

17. *Geography time: In which state is Chancellorsville?*

18. *Sherman's March to the Sea included the burning of what city?*

19. *Find one spy.*

20. *Can you name a Civil War nurse?*

21. *Who assassinated Abraham Lincoln?*

22. *Name two black soldiers.*

23. *Find three rebel generals.*

24. *Find three Union generals.*

From *The Persona Book.* © 1997. Katherine Lallier and Nancy Marino. TIP. (800) 237-6124.

Team Members' Names: _____

THE CIVIL WAR SCAVENGER HUNT
(continued)

25. *HORSE SENSE. Match the following soldiers to their favorite horse.*

    Grant   Lexington and Sam

    Lee   Daniel Webster

    Sheridan   Cincinnati

    Sherman   Traveller

    McClellan   Winchester

BONUS QUESTION

A. *Robert E. Lee said, "He has lost his left arm, but I have lost my right."*

   About whom was General Lee speaking?

B. *Abraham Lincoln said, "I can't spare this man. He fights!"*

   To whom was President Lincoln referring?

SCORE YOURSELF

1-5 correct: Private, you were probably killed at Bull Run.

6-10 correct: Add a stripe, corporal. You were probably captured and confined to Andersonville Prison.

11-15 correct: You've been commissioned a lieutenant but are wounded at Shiloh.

16-20 correct: As a cavalry captain, you survived Gettysburg

21-24 correct: As a colonel, you were present at Appomattox Courthouse

Bonus Question: Congratulations! You've achieved the rank of Major General.

Horse Sense: Give yourself a general's star for every correct answer.

From *The Persona Book.* © 1997. Katherine Lallier and Nancy Marino. TIP. (800) 237-6124.

ANSWER KEY

1. Alabama, Arkansas, Florida, Georgia, Louisiana, Mississippi, North Carolina, South Carolina, Tennessee, Texas, Virginia
2. States: California, Connecticut, Delaware, Illinois, Indiana, Iowa, Kansas, Kentucky, Maine, Maryland, Massachusetts, Michigan, Minnesota, Missouri, New Hampshire, New Jersey, New York, Ohio, Oregon, Pennsylvania, Rhode Island, Vermont, and Wisconsin. Territories: Colorado, Dakota, Nebraska, Nevada, New Mexico, Utah, and Washington fought on the Union side. West Virginia formed in 1863 to support the Union. The border states Maryland, Missouri, and Kentucky had people fighting on both sides of the war, but their governments were Union.
3. James Buchanan
4. Harriet Tubman, Harriet Beecher Stowe
5. Harriet Beecher Stowe
6. Jefferson Davis
7. Answers might include Harriet Tubman, John Brown, Harriet Beecher Stowe
8. John Brown
9. Fort Sumter
10. Two
11. *Monitor* and *Merrimack*
12. September 17, 1862
13. Unconditional Surrender
14. At the Battle of Bull Run, he would not budge from his position—like a stone wall.
15. Four score and seven years ago
16. Pennsylvania
17. Virginia
18. Atlanta
19. Answers might include Belle Boyd, Elizabeth Van Lew, Rose O'Neal Greenhow
20. Answers might include Clara Barton, Mary Anne Bickerdyke, Dorothea Dix
21. John Wilkes Booth
22. Answers might include Robert Smalls, William Carney, Christian Fleetwood, Lewis Douglass
23. Answers might include Lee, Jackson, Longstreet, Beauregard
24. Answers might include Grant, Sherman, McClellan, McDowell
25. Grant = Cincinnati
    Lee = Traveller
    Sheridan = Winchester
    Sherman = Lexington and Sam
    McClellan = Daniel Webster

Bonus Voices:

A. Stonewall Jackson
B. Ulysses S. Grant

For your debate, you need not use Abraham Lincoln and Stephen Douglas. Any Northerner can argue against any Southern persona effectively. The abolitionists can also argue with one another about the methods of ending slavery.

Slavery is not the only possible issue for debate, however. The Civil War primarily dealt with the issue of states' rights versus a central federal government—a monumental debate that still has great relevance. Phrase your issue as follows: The rights of individual states are more important than a powerful central government.

To conduct a formal debate in your classroom, use the style of debate known as the Lincoln-Douglas debate. It was named in honor of the pair who used this form more than a century ago. The affirmative, or pro position, speaks first. The negative, or con position, follows. The affirmative position is then given time for rebuttal. If only two students are involved in the debate, this style will work well.

Roundtable Regiment Discussion Groups

It is important that you allow your regiments time to work together as a group. They need to know how they are alike and different from the other members of their regiment. Students should share the information they gather. They must discuss it as it relates to their persona. It is also extremely important that they discuss their thoughts and research in the first person. They should not be saying Sarah Edmonds dressed as a Union soldier to fight for the North, rather," *I* wanted to fight for the Union, but I was a woman. *I* decided to dress as a man to defend my cause." Becoming comfortable with speaking in the first person will aid the students who take part in the *tableaux-vivants*, the Who Am I? epitaphs, the dramas, and every other activity in this unit.

Conduct a roundtable regiment discussion group with each of your groups. After they have researched their personas and the Civil War, present the groups with pointed questions about their individual roles in the war. Discuss the mural they created and why they chose it. This activity will bring in all the higher-order thinking skills of Bloom's taxonomy—analysis, synthesis, and evaluation (see page 2). Students will analyze, synthesize, and evaluate their persona's role in the Civil War.

In one such discussion group, the child who chose the persona of Robert E. Lee was asked what he thought his greatest victory of the war was. After a moment of consideration he answered, "I would have to say Chancellorsville was my greatest victory, but it was also my greatest defeat. It was there I lost Stonewall Jackson. He was a great general, and he was my friend."

The student who portrayed Lee analyzed the information he gathered and made a judgment on the facts. Although his opinion is debatable, he had concrete evidence to support his views. This boy understood the character of Lee and truly felt a connection to him through the persona project.

As children prepare to take part in the roundtable discussion groups, you may want to assign a particular Civil War historical fiction or biography to each regiment. There are many excellent novels on the war and Reconstruction. Consider using the following titles if you wish to incorporate a book discussion and add another literature component to your study of the war. (See the bibliography on page 154 for more information on specific books.)

B. Activities and Games

Red Cross Voices: Shura's *Gentle Annie: The True Story of a Civil War Nurse*, or Lyon's *Here and Then*. The latter book incorporates time travel as a present-day reenactor helps a Civil War nurse get needed supplies. Wisler's *Mr. Lincoln's Drummer* includes scenes of the wounded on the front line and in hospitals.

Abolitionist Voices: Rappaport's *Escape from Slavery: Five Journeys to Freedom*, Hamilton's *Many Thousand Gone: African Americans from Slavery to Freedom*, or the McKissacks' *Christmas in the Big House, Christmas in the Quarters*. All three books show the harsh reality of slave life and the role of the Underground Railroad.

Voices of the South: Reeder's *Shades of Gray* is the story of a Southern boy whose family is wiped out during the war. He is forced to live with his cowardly uncle, who refused to fight for the Confederacy. Slowly, he learns to understand his uncle's point of view. Climo's *A Month of Seven Days* shows a young Southern girl's fear of the Yankees who occupy her home during the war. The McKissacks' *Christmas in the Big House, Christmas in the Quarters* shows the striking contrast between slaves' and masters' lives.

Rebel Voices: Beatty's *Eben Tyne, Powdermonkey* is a fictional account of life aboard the great Southern ironclad, Merrimack. Reeder's *Shades of Gray* and Climo's *A Month of Seven Days* also define the feelings of the Confederacy.

Voice of the Black Soldiers: Cooper's *From Slave to Civil War Hero: The Life and Times of Robert Smalls* tells the adventurous tale of the ex-slave who captured the boat *Planter* for the Union.

Union Voices: Wisler's *Mr. Lincoln's Drummer* is a factually based book on the 3rd Vermont regiment from the point of view of the 11-year-old drummer boy who received the Medal of Honor. Beatty's highly acclaimed *Charley Skedaddle* tells of a New York City boy who joins the Union after his brother is killed at Gettysburg. Both books depict the reality of battle from the foot soldier's point of view.

Voice of the Women Soldiers: Stevens's *Frank Thompson: Her Civil War Story* tells the story of female soldier Sarah Edmonds before, during, and after the war.

The Presidents' Voices: Wisler's *Mr. Lincoln's Drummer* portrays the feelings of Lincoln about the war. *Lincoln, in His Own Words* gives insight about the 16th president from his own writings.

A Voice with a Picture: Wisler's *Mr. Lincoln's Drummer* includes a sketch artist as a supporting character. The character of Julian Scott goes on to become a war correspondent. Sullivan's *Mathew Brady: His Life and Photographs* is another book about the most famous photographer of the era.

CIVIL WAR WORD SCRAMBLE

There are many words and phrases that originated or became popular during the Civil War. Here are a few that have been jumbled in this word scramble.

1. General Burnside made a fashion statement by growing these on the side of his face. **DEBRISSUN**

2. Unless you wanted to be shot and killed, you would not cross this line at Andersonville prison. **LEENADDI**

3. Civil War surgeons were also known by this nickname, which was a reference to the great number of amputations performed. **WEBANOSS**

4. Lincoln proclaimed this day a national holiday in late 1864. **SKINTHVINGAG**

5. This kind of hollering made the Confederate troops famous. **ERLEB LELY**

6. Originally it referred to the stringing together of a series of pup tents. But it has become a slang expression that means the whole thing. **HANSGEB**

7. This is an expression that meant a person, not the animal, had plain common sense. **SHORE SNEES**

8. If you go to the candy store, you will find this kind of nutty candy. It was the slang word for peanuts. **BROOGES**

9. During the war, this referred to a soldier's sewing kit, not his beloved back home. **SIWUFOHEE**

10. If you have run away in a hurry, you may have been asked to do this. **EKLADEDDS**

ANSWER KEY:

1. Sideburns	6. Shebang
2. Deadline	7. Horse sense
3. Sawbones	8. Goobers
4. Thanksgiving	9. Housewife
5. Rebel Yell	10. Skedaddle

From *The Persona Book*. © 1997. Katherine Lallier and Nancy Marino. TIP. (800) 237-6124.

C. Displays

Cyclorama

A cyclorama is a large, panoramic mural that encircles a room. During the 1800s, going to a cyclorama was a popular form of entertainment. People would view the elaborate, circular murals. One famous cyclorama is on display at Gettysburg National Military Park. It was painted by Paul Dominique Philippoteaux and is called "The High Tide of the Confederacy: July 3, 1863." It depicts the battlefield during the last confrontation between the confederate forces of Robert E. Lee and the Union Army lead by George Meade.

Use mural paper and have students create a large, circular mural around the classroom or library. This project can be easily downsized by using a ream of computer paper.

Persona Epitaphs

Whether they died in battle or many years after the war, every individual who had a personal role in the Civil War is long gone. Their voices have been silenced by time. The last messages left by many appear as epitaphs, which are inscriptions on a tombstone in memory of a deceased person. In some cases the epitaph was written by the deceased before his or her death. Many times it was written by friends and family members as a commentary on their beloved's life. An epitaph might include the deceased's contributions, a quote, or an ideal to live by, or it may simply list factual information.

Although all the personas who are included in this unit actually existed and may have inscriptions at their grave sites already, students should be given the opportunity to write original epitaphs. After learning about their personas' roles in the Civil War, students should synthesize this information and create a tombstone. Basic information such as dates

and places can be included as well as major contributions or aspirations. Use the sample epitaphs to guide children in creating ones for their personas.

Tombstones can be cut from gray construction paper with the epitaph appearing on one side. On the reverse side, students can include their "Who Am I" research on their character written in the first person.

SAMPLE EPITAPHS OF FAMOUS AMERICANS

Thomas Jefferson

Here was buried
Thomas Jefferson
author of the
Declaration of Independence
and of the
Statute of Virginia
for Religious Freedom
and Father of the
University of Virginia
Born: April 12, 1743
Died: July 4, 1826

George Washington

To the Memory of the Man,
First in war,
First in peace,
and First in the hearts of his countrymen

Will Rogers

I never met a man I didn't like

Unknown Soldier

Here rests in
Honored Glory
An American Soldier
Known but to God
1941-1945 (WWII) 1950-1953 (Korea) 1958-1975 (Vietnam)

Benjamin Franklin

The body of
B. Franklin Printer
(Like the Cover of an old Book
Its Contents worn out
And stript of its Lettering and Gilding)
Lies here, Food for Worms
But the Work shall not be lost,
For it will (as he believ'd) appear once more
In a new and more elegant Edition
Revised and corrected
by the Author.

Martin Luther King Jr.

Free at Last, Free at Last
Thank God Almighty
I'm Free at Last

Civil War Memorial

Create a Civil War memorial by combining the epitaphs with the persona "Who Am I?" work sheets. Have students place the epitaph on one side of gray paper and the work sheet and an illustration of their persona on the other. Display the memorial on a bulletin board with green paper in the background or hang from "clotheslines" that cross your room.

D. Spectacles

The Grand Review

In May 1865, more than 150,000 men marched in Washington, D.C. The volunteer armies of the Potomac, the Tennessee, and the Georgia all marched in front of the president and his generals before being disbanded.

For a culminating activity, create your own grand review. Have your regiments march in costume around the school. Invite parents or other grades to be the viewing committee. After the parade, have your regiments take their places in the *tableaux-vivants* or in a performance. This way students can share with everyone their knowledge of the Civil War.

The Battle of Bull Run, First Manassas

If you have visited any of the Civil War battlefields, you may be familiar with reenactors. These are men and women who attempt to re-create history by dressing and behaving as their historical counterparts. The climax is usually a battle simulation.

When children are introduced to the idea of becoming the personas of the Civil War, their first thoughts frequently are drawn to the great battles. They tend to see war in romantic and glorious terms. As teachers it is our goal to educate students about the brutality and inhumanity of war. However, the Civil War was made up of a series of violent battles. People died and homes were destroyed. It would be unrealistic to present the war without a battle scene.

For this reason, the first Battle of Bull Run, also known as First Manassas, was chosen. It was the first major battle of the war. Until this moment, Northerners and Southerners thought the war would be a picnic. Indeed, actual picnickers came to watch at a nearby bluff. Both sides thought the war would be over in three months and that the amount of blood shed would "fill a thimble." It was at Bull Run that both sides learned the truth about war.

VOICES OF THE CIVIL WAR

Characters:

For the South:
General Pierre Beauregard
General Barnard Bee*
Colonel Jubal Anderson Early
General Joseph Johnston*
Narrator*
Three picnickers*
Three Union soldiers*

For the North:
Kady Brownell (flag bearer)
General Irvin McDowell
Captain James Ricketts*

Everyone involved in the Civil War unit will participate in the battle. With the exception of the aforementioned personas, all other students will divide into Union and Confederate soldiers. A small group of picnickers will be commenting on what they see. Extra soldiers may be added by inviting another class to participate with yours. These students need not be grade-level partners. Drop down a grade, and have your students "mentor" younger children. The number of students participating will determine actual battle maneuvers. Students need to be told if they will shoot or be shot and by whom. If you are working with a group of 20 or fewer, students may have to be resurrected from their mortal wounds to continue to battle.

Setting: Manassas, Virginia. Sunday, July 21, 1861. There is a small river known as Bull Run, and Stone Bridge crosses over it. In the background is Henry House Hill—there is an actual Henry House on the hill. On an eastern hill, a crowd of spectators prepare their picnic lunches.

NARRATOR: Welcome to Manassas, Virginia. Today's date is Sunday, July 21, 1861, and boy, is it hot already. Today is a most important day. The Union is going to put down those rebellious Southerners once and for all. Three months ago they had the nerve to capture Fort Sumter for themselves. Mr. Lincoln has sent General Irvin McDowell here today to capture General Beauregard's army. Everybody knows about it. That's why those folks over there brought there picnic lunches. They're going to watch the whole show.

PICNICKER #1: What a lovely day for a battle. When do you suppose they're going to start?

PICNICKER #2: According to the newspapers, it should have started already. I do hope they don't call the whole thing off. I'd hate to miss the war.

* Denotes characters not listed on the persona list. They may be added to the list, or a student should be assigned this part as well as his chosen persona.

From *The Persona Book.* © 1997. Katherine Lallier and Nancy Marino. TIP. (800) 237-6124.

D. Spectacles: The Battle of Bull Run, First Manassas

PICNICKER #3: The way I understand it, if you're not here today, you won't see anything. This should all be over with by the time we're ready to pack our things and go home.

PICNICKER #1: Pass the salt, please. This chicken is a little dry.

NARRATOR: Meanwhile, in the Northern camp, things sounded something like this....

GENERAL IRVIN McDOWELL: Captain Ricketts, ready your guns. We are going to surprise the rebels by attacking Stone Bridge now.

CAPTAIN JAMES RICKETTS: Yes, General. The soldiers are as ready as they can be, considering their lack of experience.

(Union troops begin marching to Stone Bridge. The recorded sound of gunfire fills the room, and soldiers fall to the ground.)

NARRATOR: The rebels were surprised, but General Beauregard takes command of his troops.

GENERAL PIERRE BEAUREGARD: We must launch a flank attack at the Yankees at once! Where on earth is General Johnston? Take these orders to General Bee, Colonel.

COLONEL JUBAL ANDERSON EARLY: I'm on my way, General. *(Early, a cavalryman, rides out to Bee.) (To Bee)* Here are the orders from General Beauregard.

(All the while, Union troops are on the offensive and are battering the Confederates. Both armies are extremely inexperienced. Beauregard's strategy eludes them. Troops with little experience understand one maneuver: Follow the flag.)

GENERAL BARNARD BEE: These Yankees keep pressing forward. Our men are scattering all over the place! General Johnston, you've arrived! What are we going to do?

GENERAL JOSEPH JOHNSTON: The Yankees are going after Henry House Hill. We need to gather our troops!

From *The Persona Book.* © 1997. Katherine Lallier and Nancy Marino. TIP. (800) 237-6124.

BEE: (*Seeing Jackson, seated on his horse, calmly directing the Virginia brigade*) There is Jackson standing like a stone wall! Rally behind the Virginians!

(*At that moment, General Barnard Bee is shot and killed. The Confederates begin to gather and push the Yankees back.*)

NARRATOR: This was a turning point in the battle. General Bee was shot dead but not before he gave General Thomas Jackson his nickname: Stonewall Jackson. The Confederates rallied behind the Virginians, and the battle turned in their favor. The rebels were beginning to win.

PICNICKER #2: It's so hard to tell who's who. I thought the rebels wore gray and the Yankees wore blue.

PICNICKER #3: In a perfect war, you would be right. But not everybody is wearing a matching uniform. There's a group of Union boys from Wisconsin wearing gray. I saw them marching through the streets of Washington on their way here.

PICNICKER #1: And over there, are those rebels wearing blue?

PICNICKER #2: If we cannot tell them apart, how are the soldiers supposed to?

PICNICKER #3: That's what the flags are for. Follow the flags.

PICNICKER #1: Would anyone like some watermelon?

NARRATOR: Meanwhile, back at the front, a group of Union soldiers start shooting another group of Union soldiers. It's a case of mistaken identity. You see, the soldiers who are being fired upon are wearing gray, not blue.

(*Blue Union soldiers are shooting the gray Union soldiers until Kady Brownell steps out and waves the regiment's flag furiously.*)

KADY BROWNELL: Stop! Don't you see? We're not the enemy! See our flag! Here are our colors! Stop shooting!

(*The blue soldiers stop shooting and try to offer help to the wounded and dying who were caught in the "friendly fire."*)

NARRATOR: There was another case of mistaken identity later in the day.

D. Spectacles: The Battle of Bull Run, First Manassas

UNION SOLDIER #1: Fire the cannon!

UNION SOLDIER #2: No. Look. They're wearing blue. They must be Yankees!

UNION SOLDIER #3: I've never seen them before. I think they might be rebels in blue!

(Blue Confederate soldiers come screaming their "Rebel yell." They kill the three Union men.)

NARRATOR: It's late in the day, and the Yankees have been hit hard by the Rebels' second wind. McDowell decides it's time to retreat. In army terms, this does not mean running away. It is an orderly withdrawal of troops who will return to fight another day. Unfortunately, McDowell's men are not experienced soldiers who know how to retreat in an orderly fashion. To the spectators on the hill, it looks like they're running for their lives.

PICNICKER #1: It looks like our Union boys are running away!

PICNICKER #2: I think they're heading this way!

PICNICKER #3: I think we had better run for our lives! The rebels are coming after us!

PICNICKER #1: Oh no! The rebels blew up a wagon! The road is blocked!

PICNICKER #2: We're going to be stampeded by our own side!

PICNICKER #3: Run for your lives, everyone! Run for your lives!

(The Union troops exit, leaving their dead behind.)

NARRATOR: In one day of fighting, almost 5,000 men were lost in the battle. The Confederates lost 1,982 soldiers. The Union counted 2,896 men wounded or killed. The war would rage on for four more years. In the end, the Civil War would claim 623,026 American lives.

Bibliography

Adler, David A. *A Picture Book of Frederick Douglass*. New York: Holiday House, 1993.

An American Civil War: A Multicultural Encyclopedia. Danbury, Conn.: Grolier, 1994.

Beatty, Patricia. *Charley Skedaddle*. New York: William Morrow, 1987.

———. *Eben Tyne, Powdermonkey*. New York: Morrow Junior Books, 1990.

Boatner, Mark Mayo. *The Civil War Dictionary*. New York: David McKay, 1959.

Brown, Warren. *Robert E. Lee*. New York: Chelsea House, 1992.

Burchard, Peter. *Charlotte Forten: A Black Teacher in the Civil War*. New York: Crown, 1994.

Calvert, Patricia. *Bigger*. New York: Atheneum, 1994.

Canon, Jill. *Civil War Heroines*. Santa Barbara, Calif.: Bellerophon Books, 1994.

Chang, Ina. *A Separate Battle: Women and the Civil War*. New York: Lodestar, 1991.

Climo, Shirley. *A Month of Seven Days*. New York: Thomas Y. Crowell, 1987.

Colman, Penny. *Spies! Women in the Civil War*. Cincinnati, Ohio: Betterway Books, 1992.

Cooper, Michael L. *From Slave to Civil War Hero: The Life and Times of Robert Smalls*. New York: Lodestar, 1994.

Fleischman, Paul. *Bull Run*. New York: Scholastic, 1993.

Fritz, Jean. *Harriet Beecher Stowe and the Beecher Preachers*. New York: G. P. Putnam's Sons, 1994.

———. *Stonewall*. New York: G. P. Putnam's Sons, 1979.

Gauch, Patricia Lee. *Thunder at Gettysburg*. New York: Bantam Books, 1975.

Hamilton, Virginia. *Many Thousand Gone: African Americans from Slavery to Freedom*. New York: Alfred A. Knopf, 1993.

Haskins, Jim. *The Day Fort Sumter Was Fired On: A Photo History of the Civil War*. New York: Scholastic, 1995.

———. *Get on Board: The Story of the Underground Railroad*. New York: Scholastic, 1993.

Hoobler, Thomas. *Photographing History: The Career of Mathew Brady*. New York: G. P. Putnam's Sons, 1977.

Johnson, Neil. *The Battle of Gettysburg*. New York: Four Winds Press, 1989.

Josephs, Anna Catherine. *Mountain Boy*. Milwaukee, Wis.: Raintree, 1985.

Kent, Zachary. *Jefferson Davis*. Chicago: Childrens Press, 1993.

———. *The Story of Ford's Theater and the Death of Lincoln*. Chicago: Childrens Press, 1987.

———. *The Story of Sherman's March to the Sea*. Chicago: Childrens Press, 1987.

Lyon, George Ella. *Cecil's Journey*. New York: Orchard, 1991.

———. *Here and Then*. New York: Orchard, 1994.

Marrin, Albert. *Unconditional Surrender: U. S. Grant and the Civil War*. New York: Atheneum, 1994.

———. *Virginia's General: Robert E. Lee and the Civil War*. New York: Atheneum, 1994.

McKissack, Patricia C., and Frederick L. McKissack. *Christmas in the Big House, Christmas in the Quarters*. New York: Scholastic, 1994.

Meltzer, Milton, ed. *Lincoln, in His Own Words*. New York: Harcourt Brace and Company, 1993.

———. *Voices from the Civil War: A Documentary History of the Great American Conflict*. New York: Thomas Y. Crowell, 1989.

Mettger, Zak. *Reconstruction: America After the Civil War*. New York: Lodestar, 1994.

———. *Till Victory Is Won: Black Soldiers in the Civil War*. New York: Lodestar, 1994.

Murphy, Jim. *The Boy's War: Confederate and Union Soldiers Talk About the War*. New York: Clarion Books, 1990.

O'Brien, Steven. *Ulysses S. Grant*. New York: Chelsea House, 1991.

Polacco, Patricia. *Pink and Say*. New York: Philomel, 1994.

Rappaport, Doreen. *Escape from Slavery: Five Journeys to Freedom*. New York: HarperCollins, 1991.

Ray, Delia. *Behind the Blue and Gray: The Soldier's Life in the Civil War*. New York: Lodestar, 1991.

Reeder, Carolyn. *Shades of Gray*. New York: Avon Books, 1989.

Reef, Caroline. *Civil War Soldiers*. New York: Twenty-First Century Books, 1993.

Ringgold, Faith. *Aunt Harriet's Underground Railroad in the Sky*. New York: Crown, 1992.

Robertson, James I. *Civil War! America Becomes One Nation*. New York: Alfred A. Knopf, 1992.

Shorto, Russell. *David Farragut and the Great Naval Blockade*. Columbus, Ohio: Silver Burdett, 1991.

Shura, Mary Francis. *Gentle Annie: The True Story of a Civil War Nurse*. New York: Scholastic, 1991.

Stevens, Bryna. *Frank Thompson: Her Civil War Story*. New York: Macmillan, 1992.

Stowe, Harriet Beecher. *Uncle Tom's Cabin*. New York: Coward-McCann, 1929.

Sullivan, George. *Mathew Brady: His Life and Photographs*. New York: Cobblehill Books, 1994.

Tilton, Rafael. *Clara Barton*. San Diego, Calif.: Lucent Books, 1995.

Wisler, G. Clifton. *Mr. Lincoln's Drummer*. New York: Lodestar, 1995.

Zeinert, Karen. *Elizabeth Van Lew: Southern Belle, Union Spy*. Columbus, Ohio.: Silver Burdett, 1995.

Video Recordings

Abraham Lincoln. Atlas Video, Inc., 1990. 30 min. videocassette. Distrib. by Library Video Company. (800) 843-3620.

Civil War Generals: Robert E. Lee. Atlas Video, Inc., 1989. 30 min. videocassette. Distrib. by Library Video Company. (800) 843-3620.

Civil War Generals: Ulysses S. Grant. Atlas Video, Inc., 1989. 30 min. videocassette. Distrib. by Library Video Company. (800) 843-3620.

Follow the Drinking Gourd: A Story of the Underground Railroad. Rabbit Ears Productions, 1992. 30 min. videocassette. Distrib. by Library Video Company. (800) 843-3620.

Touring Civil War Battlefields. Questar Video Inc., 1988. 60 min. videocassette. Distrib. by Library Video Company. (800) 843-3620.

5 American Heroes for Our Times

Defining America as a Nation Through the Attributes of Outstanding Americans

Table of Contents

Biography Personas	158
Step One: Prepersona Activities	161
Step Two: Decision Making	162
Step Three: Discovery Period	162
Culminating Activities	165
A. Dramas	167
B. Activities and Games	179
C. Displays	186
D. Spectacles	189
Bibliography	190

American Heroes for Our Times

Biography: the study of people. Discovering what makes certain people outstanding and notable is essentially what a biography is all about. This chapter is the study of real people, specifically real Americans, who affected our national character. They are people with attributes worth learning about and learning from. It is a study of heroes in a time that sorely lacks or downplays admirable people. All the people selected—some old familiar faces, others overlooked by traditional history—share one thing in common: They are from America, which includes Mexico and Canada.

We chose familiar faces such as Abraham Lincoln, George Washington Carver, and Amelia Earhart because their lives can be easily researched in most classrooms and libraries. The lesser-known people we chose—including Princess Ka'iulani, Matthew Henson, and Susan LaFlesche Picotte—are the subjects of outstanding recent biographies. Finally, we chose people who symbolize certain positive attributes and who overcame a multitude of obstacles—and in so doing became role models to today's children. Together the choices represent the multicultural nature of America. Other famous people not included in this chapter can be easily added based on personal preferences and the accessibility of biographies about them. The books that have been chosen are at varying reading levels to meet the needs of all students, who may continue their persona research using such resources as almanacs, atlases, or books of quotations.

Though many activities are suggested in this chapter, you should choose only those that suit your needs and the individual nature of your class. But note that the trading-card project is a great first-year project. Exploring what qualities go into making a person a hero is an interesting perspective on learning about the genre of biography.

Biography Personas

The following group of personas is as eclectic as America itself. The people covered—from those living during the time of Pocahontas to the periods of the Revolutionary, Civil, and World Wars to the present—can best be described as unique and varied. Look in the bibliography (pages 190-192) for recommended books.

Alvin Ailey: This inventive, spirited choreographer started his own dance company in New York City.

Louisa May Alcott: Author of the timeless classic *Little Women*, Alcott was a teacher, author, and fighter for women's rights.

Benedict Arnold: Instead of becoming—as he had hoped—a leader and a hero, Arnold became the most famous traitor in American history. He has been included in this study of heroes to offer contrast and to allow students to learn from negative attributes. His story is told in Fritz's *Traitor: The Case of Benedict Arnold*.

Arthur Ashe: A trailblazer in the all-white world of tennis, Ashe was the only African American to ever attain the number-one ranking on the men's tennis tour.

Benjamin Banneker: An intellectual leader during Revolutionary times, Banneker was an astronomer, a farmer, a mathematician, and a surveyor. He was also one of the first American blacks to publicly denounce slavery.

Henry Bergh: His personal courage enabled him to establish the American Society for the Prevention of Cruelty to Animals in 1866.

Mary McLeod Bethune: This well-known educator fought for equal schooling for blacks and whites.

Nellie Bly: The pseudonym for a journalist whose real name was Elizabeth Cochrane Seaman who did undercover news investigations that exposed many social injustices.

Frances Hodgson Burnett: This best-selling author wrote more than 60 books, including *The Secret Garden, Little Lord Fauntleroy,* and *A Little Princess.*

Cesar Chavez: His fight was for human rights and dignity for migrant workers and farm workers.

Crazy Horse: This great Sioux warrior defeated General Custer in the battle of Little Bighorn.

Benjamin Davis: The fourth African American to graduate from West Point—the first in the twentieth century—Benjamin Davis Jr. commanded the country's first group of African American combat pilots.

Amelia Earhart: A famous aviator, Earhart broke many world flying records.

George Eastman: He revolutionized photography when he invented an easier way to take pictures.

Matthew Henson: This Arctic explorer was the only African American to accompany Admiral Peary on his excursion to the North Pole.

Milton Hershey: He made a fortune from his boyhood passion: candy.

Sam Houston: This colorful frontiersman was the commander in chief of the Texas army, the first president of the Texas Republic, the governor of Texas, and a U.S. congressman.

Mary Harris Jones: "Mother Jones" fought for the rights of children factory workers and other mistreated laborers.

Chief Joseph: This Nez Percé warrior led Native Americans to victory in one of the greatest battles against the U.S. Army.

Princess Ka'iulani: Hawaii's last princess, the princess was denied her right to the throne when the monarchy was abolished.

Martin Luther King Jr.: This slain civil-rights leader fought for peaceful change.

Abraham Lincoln: Legendary president during the Civil War.

Wilma Mankiller: She was the first woman to become the principal chief of the Cherokee Nation.

Elijah McCoy: This child of runaway slaves became a famous inventor.

Anna Mary Moses: "Grandma Moses" was a famous painter.

I. M. Pei: One of America's greatest architects, Pei has designed massive skyscrapers and small family homes.

Susan LaFlesche Picotte: This Omaha Indian was the first Native American woman to graduate from medical school.

Pocahontas: This Powhatan Indian will be forever linked with Jamestown, Va., and Captain John Smith.

Colin Powell: This proud, confident American became a member of the joint chiefs of staff of the U.S. Armed Forces in 1989.

Diego Rivera: Instead of painting pictures for museums, this famous artist painted pictures on walls in public spaces for everyone—rich and poor.

Franklin Delano Roosevelt: Serving as the 32nd president of the United States, FDR brought the nation out of the Great Depression and into World War II.

Theodore Roosevelt: He was a conservationist, hunter, politician, president, governor, soldier, and family man.

Robert Smalls: This former slave risked his life by guiding a ship, *The Planter*, from Charleston to the Union forces.

Elizabeth Cady Stanton: She fought hard for equality for women, including the right to vote.

Tecumseh: This great Shawnee leader was a warrior and a statesman.

Henry David Thoreau: He was a poet, author, and teacher who decided to lead a simple life and moved to Walden Pond.

Harriet Tubman: She was the Underground Railroad's most famous conductor and became known as the Moses of her people.

E. B. White: This author is best known for his children's classics, *Stuart Little* and *Charlotte's Web*.

Laura Ingalls Wilder: Famous for her autobiographical series that inspired the television show "Little House on the Prairie," Wilder was a pioneer girl who endured many hardships.

Edith Wilson: She became the first lady when her second husband, Woodrow Wilson, became president of the United States.

Chuck Yeager: He is one of America's most accomplished pilots and was the first to break the sound barrier.

Step One: Prepersona Activities

1. There are many interesting picture biographies to read aloud to your class. See the bibliography (pages 190-192) for more information on these books.

   Stanley's *The Last Princess: The Story of Princess Ka'iulani of Hawaii* tells the story of the tragic life of Hawaii's last heir to the throne. It is beautifully illustrated and rich in text. Other choices include Giblin's *George Washington: A Picture Book Biography* and *Thomas Jefferson: A Picture Book Biography*. Finally, for a large selection of personalities done in one format, try Adler's series, which includes *A Picture Book of Harriet Tubman* among others.

2. After reading several biographies to your class, discuss with your students the nature of a biography. Include the traditional discussion of dates, childhood experiences, and impact on history. Discuss parallel events occurring during the person's life or problems of society that influenced this hero. Be sure to emphasize the positive characteristics or attributes that helped shape this person.

3. Familiarize students with the heroes about whom they will be reading.

   One method is to explore two of Provensen's books: *The Buck Stops Here* and *My Fellow Americans*. These incredible "coffee-table" books for kids are deceptively simple in appearance but contain a great deal of background. *The Buck Stops Here* is a pictorial jump-rope rhyme that includes presidents from George Washington through George Bush. Stop on any page, and you are drawn in by the wealth of information. Children can be encouraged to update the book with new rhymes and illustrations for Bill Clinton and "all to come."

   My Fellow Americans is an even greater undertaking. Provensen pays tribute to a multitude of Americans—all deceased—by grouping them in a variety of categories, such as Free Spirits, Ecologists, Pathfinders, Guiding Lights, and even Expatriates. The illustrated feast for the eyes is punctuated with a quotation illuminating the group. This book is a great discussion book, especially if there are several copies available for students to study more closely.

   An interesting way of introducing students to the biography collection is to have a scavenger hunt in the library. A general one is included in this chapter. By examining the biography section of your own library, students become familiar with the biographical genre and the heroes they will be studying. Encourage students to work in pairs or groups to complete the scavenger hunt in a library period.

4. Develop a strategy to introduce children to role-playing: Read Burleigh's *Flight: The Journey of Charles Lindbergh* aloud to your class. To encourage children to start thinking in the first person, ask them the following questions. Their responses may be written or oral.

   Charles Lindbergh kept a diary of his famous journey. What if you were Charles Lindbergh? What would you write in your diary? How would you feel about flying across the ocean? What would you do to keep awake for such a long period of time? What attributes—personality characteristics—do you have that would help you during this voyage? What would you do to combat loneliness, or would you not be lonely? What would be the first thing you would do when you got to France?

Step Two: Decision Making

1. Explain to students they will be choosing a persona and they will be doing projects as that persona. Talk about some of the culminating projects.

2. Each student will be asked to make three choices and to give reasons why they want to be a certain character. These reasons will be important if two or more children want to be the same persona.

3. Place a copy of the "American Heroes" criteria for decision making in a visible place and give each student a copy of the criteria. Encourage children to invent additional criteria. See the next page for a copy of the decision-making form.

4. Review the list of personas. Emphasize the lesser-known characters. Have a list of personas for the students to refer to when choosing their personas.

5. Have students complete the "American Heroes" decision-making work sheet.

6. For the lesson that follows, meet with each student individually. It is especially important to talk with students who did not get their first choice, because all should be happy with their choices.

Step Three: Discovery Period

During this period students read their biographies and start to gather information about their persona. Have a biography readathon on a day or an afternoon set aside for reading. Allow students to bring in snacks and blankets. Let them get comfortable and "curl up with their really good books."

Encourage students to learn not only about their own personas but about the period of American history in which they lived. Students should examine at least five world events that took place during their persona's lifetime. Some events may have had a direct impact on the lives of their personas; other times the effect may have been more subtle. For example, the Civil War had a greater effect on Abraham Lincoln than it did on Grandma Moses. As students learn about the America in which their personas lived, they can start their diaries in which they should be encouraged to write in the first person about the event.

After reading their biographies, groups of students can look for more information about their personas in various references sources. This not only helps them learn about their personas but is an opportunity to learn about various types of information sources available in their library.

Each group looks at an information source, such as an atlas or a book of records, and answers the following questions:

How is it organized?

Why would I use it?

What information is contained in the source?

Demonstrate how to use either the table of contents or the index.

How would your persona use this information source?

Name _____

AMERICAN HEROES
DECISION-MAKING WORK SHEET

DECISION: WHICH HERO DO I WANT TO BE?

ALTERNATIVES:

Your selected biography books.

DECISION:

Answer the questions on the following page, and use those answers to make a decision. Give reasons for your decision. The more thorough your answer, the more likely it is that you will receive your choice. List two alternatives as well.

Give three choices in order of preference.

1. _____

2. _____

3. _____

From *The Persona Book*. © 1997. Katherine Lallier and Nancy Marino. TIP. (800) 237-6124.

Name _____

AMERICAN HEROES
DECISION-MAKING WORK SHEET

Page 2

DECISION: WHICH AMERICAN HERO DO I WISH TO BE?

1. What do I find interesting about this person?

2. Will I enjoy reading the biography?

3. Will I do all the research necessary to investigate this persona?

4. Will I be able to design and create a costume for this person?

5. Am I willing to find out how the person made the world a better place?

From *The Persona Book.* © 1997. Katherine Lallier and Nancy Marino. TIP. (800) 237-6124.

Students then decide how they will share what they have learned with the rest of the class. Encourage creativity. Students can design a board game, create a song, make a bulletin board, or even put on a performance. Remind students that their goal is to teach others about how to use their information source.

Below are suggestions for each persona to examine:

Explorers, generals: atlas, maps

Orators, authors: Bartlett's *Familiar Quotations* or another quotation book

Reporters, politicians: newspapers, *Readers' Guide to Periodical Literature*

Athletes, world-record holders: *Guinness Book of World Records* or another record book

People who achieved a "first," inventors: *Famous First Facts*

Benjamin Franklin, Benjamin Banneker—publishers of almanacs—and other miscellaneous personas: almanac

Who Am I?

The "Who Am I?" work sheet (see page 166), assists students in creating their persona trading cards. This is one of the important culminating activities. Writing is one of the most difficult tasks that students are asked to do. In order to ease students into the creative writing process, the following questionnaire is provided. The results, written in the first person, will be included on their trading card for the Hall of Fame. The child also designs a picture of his or her persona to accompany the creative writing.

Culminating Activities

A talk show complete with commercials and a living museum are just some of the culminating activities for students' American-hero personas. The talk show allows students to tell their persona's story. The living museum is a collection of displays and games that center on these heroes.

Below are the types of culminating activities for this unit. Select a limited number of activities.

Dramas. Choose dramas if you and your students wish to perform. The skits on the following pages provide a basic outline. Have your students enhance these skits or create their own.

Activities and Games. These are interactive games and activities that can be prepared for the Living Museum. These games help a students learn more about their personas.

Displays. The displays and demonstrations are perfect ways to transform your classroom, library, or school auditorium into an American Hero Hall of Fame.

Spectacles. Spectacles are activities that are performed in front of an audience. They differ from dramas because many students may participate in these activities. In this chapter, the spectacle is the Living Museum.

Student's Name _____

Persona's Name _____

AMERICAN HEROES FOR OUR TIMES
WHO AM I? WORK SHEET

Whether your persona is an inventor, general, politician, poet, or other hero, you must let everyone know who you are. In no fewer than five sentences, tell me about yourself.

Examples of what you might include are:

1. What did you accomplish?

2. What major historical event or events took place in the United States during your life?

3. What was your job?

4. What major obstacles did you have to overcome?

5. How would you describe yourself: Some choices: brave, shy, mysterious, clever, ruthless, heroic, fearless, curious, confident, smart, dedicated, loyal, humble, evil, honest, powerful, smart, sly, fair.

From *The Persona Book*. © 1997. Katherine Lallier and Nancy Marino. TIP. (800) 237-6124.

A. Dramas

A talk show encourages the students to synthesize and analyze all they have learned about their persona. They must have knowledge of the person and the historical period in which they lived. Use the following performance as a guide or have your students think up their own questions for each persona.

TIME LINE USA
THE TALK SHOW

Characters:
Louisa May Alcott
Benjamin Davis Jr.
Amelia Earhart
Matthew Henson
Abraham Lincoln
Pocahontas
Diego Rivera
Teddy Roosevelt
Harriet Tubman

TEDDY: *(Backstage)* Live, from the North Pole, it's Time Line USA, starring that incredible arctic explorer, Matthew Henson!

(Curtain opens.)

MATT: Thank you, Teddy. And let's hear it for Teddy Roosevelt's fabulous band, the Rough Riders. According to the *TV Guide*, today's show was supposed to be about people who look like their pets, but we're preempting it to bring you the following special.

It's quite rare to get the following people all in the same city much less the same century. So we hope you enjoy the show.

Today's topic for discussion will be "Does America Have Any Real Heroes?" Do the young people of this country have anyone they can admire?

Before we get started, I just wanted to know: Teddy, where did you get your incredible tan?

TEDDY: Same as always, Matt. I was charging up San Juan Hill. Right now I'd like to introduce our first guest, the incredibly lovely Powhatan princess, Pocahontas. *(Clapping)*

(Enter Pocahontas)

MATT: Pocahontas, it's been too long—over 300 years, is it?

From *The Persona Book.* © 1997. Katherine Lallier and Nancy Marino. TIP. (800) 237-6124.

POCAHONTAS:	Entirely too long, but rescuing John Smith and keeping the peace keeps me busy.
MATT:	Speaking of John Smith, how is he doing?
POCAHONTAS:	Actually, I haven't seen Mr. Smith in quite a while. I went on a tour of Europe and met my husband, John Rolfe.
MATT:	You mean you and John Smith didn't tie the knot?
POCAHONTAS:	I don't know why everyone asks me that. Oh well, legend is one thing, history is quite another.
MATT:	Pocahontas, it was great to have you but I see we have to go to a commercial. Stay tuned, we'll be back after a word from our sponsor.

COMMERCIAL #1 (See "The Commercials," which follows.)

TEDDY:	Matt, you're going to be excited about our next two guests. We have with us the founder of the Underground Railroad and our 16th president. Please give a warm welcome to Harriet Tubman and Abraham Lincoln.

(Enter Harriet and Abe)

MATT:	Before I say anything else, I want the two of you to know how much I've admired all the work you've done in ending slavery.
HARRIET:	Thank you, Matt. But our work is far from over. Our goal now is to promote peace and understanding among everyone. I cannot rest until there is harmony among all people.
MATT:	You're quite a lady, Mrs. Tubman. Mr. Lincoln, you've been out of the political arena for quite some time. Now, tell me, what do you think of our current president?
ABE:	Well, the jury is still out on him because he is fairly new to the job.
MATT:	Mr. Lincoln, would you consider running against him in the upcoming election?

From *The Persona Book*. © 1997. Katherine Lallier and Nancy Marino. TIP. (800) 237-6124.

ABE: I think we should leave it to the good people of this country.

(Matt asks audience for their opinion.)

MATT: We'll be right back after this commercial.

COMMERCIAL #2

TEDDY: Welcome back. Matt, our next two guests have gained fame from the arts. First, please give a warm welcome to that best-selling author, Louisa May Alcott.

(Enter Louisa)

MATT: Louisa, you look stunning. I picked up your latest book and I couldn't put it down.

LOUISA: Thank you, Matt. You know, I based a lot of what *Little Women* is about on my own life. The character of Jo March is really me.

MATT: You mean to say that you think that women are equal to men?

LOUISA: Absolutely, anyone who buys a copy of *Little Women* will see how strongly I feel about women's rights.

MATT: I wish I could discuss this further, but I see time is short. Teddy, who's our next guest?

TEDDY: Straight from creating a mural on a building in New York City is artist Diego Rivera.

(Enter Diego)

MATT: I'm not sure our audience is familiar with your work. Could you describe where you get the ideas for your paintings?

DIEGO: I paint what I see. Since I was a small boy in Mexico, I have always drawn what moves me—whether good or bad.

From *The Persona Book.* © 1997. Katherine Lallier and Nancy Marino. TIP. (800) 237-6124.

MATT:	Your art is emotional, but I have one serious problem with your murals. Why don't you paint for museums on canvas instead of painting on walls? Would you consider what you do graffiti?
DIEGO:	I draw on the walls so that the poor people can enjoy my art. It is my intention to educate people through my art.
MATT:	Well, let's ask our studio audience. Is mural painting on city walls art or graffiti?

(Matt asks audience for their opinion.)

MATT:	We'll be right back after these messages.

COMMERCIAL #3

TEDDY:	Welcome back. Our next guest is the first woman to fly across the Atlantic. Please welcome Amelia Earhart. *(Pause)* Please welcome Amelia Earhart. *(Pause)* Amelia Earhart.
MATT:	Teddy, she did get the plane reservations, right?
TEDDY:	No, she insisted on flying herself.
AMELIA:	*(From the audience carrying a plane wing)* Over here, Matt. I'm coming. *(Gets onstage)* Sorry to be so late. I had some engine trouble.
MATT:	As long as you're here. Amelia, your plane went down in 1937. What happened?
AMELIA:	A lot of people thought I was captured by the Japanese and believed to be a spy, and some people thought I was lost in the Bermuda Triangle. Actually, I ran out of gas.
MATT:	We're so happy that you could be here tonight. Teddy is signaling that we have to go to a station break. We'll be back with our last guest after these words from our sponsor.

A. Dramas: Time Line USA, The Talk Show

COMMERCIAL #4

TEDDY: Time is short, but I'd like to introduce you to our final guest, Benjamin Davis Jr., the first African American combat pilot.

MATT: It's an honor to meet with you, sir. The topic of our show is, "Does America Have Any Real Heroes?" You have always been a hero to me because of what happened to you at West Point. Could you fill in our studio audience?

BEN: Sure, Matt. My years at West Point were difficult. Because I was the first African American man in the twentieth century to attend that school, my classmates had a hard time accepting me. For the four years I was there, not one person would speak to me. I don't think of myself as a hero, but I'd stick up for something I thought was right and wouldn't give up no matter how hard it was for me.

MATT: To me, General Davis, that's what being a hero is all about. What do you say, America, Do we have heroes? (Audience applauds.)

I see we're out of time. Please join us tomorrow when the topic will be "Forty Ways to Cook Snow." You've been a great audience. Good night, everybody.

The Commercials

Throughout the dramas presented in this book, we encourage the students to enhance, rewrite, or create their own scripts. The task can seem overwhelming, especially when there is a readily available script. However, when it comes to the commercials for the talk show, your students will enjoy coming up with their own dramatizations.

The script for the commercial is easier to write because of two important factors. First, the commercial requires only two characters—though it may include more—so the dialogue is simple to construct and follow. Second, the script is short—only 30 seconds' worth of dialogue!

One of the most interesting aspects of the commercial is to pair up two famous Americans who appear to have nothing in common. They may not even have lived in the same century. The children must discover what the pair have in common and what they can advertise. Do not feel you must "pre-pair" your personas. Random pairings are often the best mix.

The commercial can sell a product or a service, or it can be a public-service announcement. The following are sample commercials that you can use as models for your students or as ready-made scripts.

COMMERCIAL #1
Public Service Announcement for the environment

Characters:
 Chief Joseph
 Crazy Horse

CHIEF JOSEPH: My name is Chief Joseph, and I am a leader of the Nez Percé people. It has been my fortune to know the majesty that is the Northwest of this great land. The grand trees and towering mountains are my brothers.

CRAZY HORSE: I am the Sioux warrior known as Crazy Horse. The glorious plains and fields are my family.

CHIEF JOSEPH: We are here to remind you that this land belongs to none of us, but we must all take care of her.

CRAZY HORSE: As I ride across this noble place now known as America, I fear for its children.

CHIEF JOSEPH: The air is clouded, the water is murky, and the land is spoiled.

CRAZY HORSE: Together, we have a common enemy: pollution.

From *The Persona Book*. © 1997. Katherine Lallier and Nancy Marino. TIP. (800) 237-6124.

CHIEF JOSEPH:	We must unite and save the environment for the present and for our future.
CRAZY HORSE:	Stop the pollution now!
CHIEF JOSEPH and CRAZY HORSE:	America: love it, or leave it!

COMMERCIAL #2
Commercial for a national book tour

Characters:
   Frances Hodgson Burnett   Laura Ingalls Wilder
   E. B. White

E. B. WHITE:	It is my pleasure to be able to speak to you today about a few good books. My name is E. B. White, and I am presently touring the country with two other authors: Laura Ingalls Wilder and Frances Hodgson Burnett.
FRANCES HODGSON BURNETT:	We've joined this book tour because we want to spread the word about reading to children.
LAURA INGALLS WILDER:	That's why we've written some books especially for the young.
WHITE:	And the young at heart. Take some of my books: *Charlotte's Web* and *Stuart Little*. They can be enjoyed by children and parents alike.
BURNETT:	The same can be said for my books *The Secret Garden* and *The Little Princess*. They're good enough to make into movies.
WILDER:	Not to mention my *Little House on the Prairie* book series. I can see it making a wonderful television show.
WHITE:	But all our stories are books first.
BURNETT:	Visit us at your local bookstore today.
WILDER:	Mention this ad, and you'll receive an extra 30-percent discount!

From *The Persona Book.* © 1997. Katherine Lallier and Nancy Marino. TIP. (800) 237-6124.

ELEVATOR UPS AND DOWNS

The following performance takes famous Americans with different viewpoints, cultures, and personalities and puts them into a common modern situation: a stuck elevator. Use this as a model, and have students create their own script. Or they may elaborate on this one. Another variation is to give students the script up to the point where the elevator stops and have them complete it. Although he is not a hero, Benedict Arnold is in this performance to provide conflict.

Characters:
Benedict Arnold   *Grandma Moses*
Nellie Bly   *Susan LaFlesche Picotte*
George Eastman   *Robert Smalls*
Milton Hershey   *Tecumseh*
Princess Ka'iulani   *Henry David Thoreau*
Margaret Mead   *Chuck Yeager*

NELLIE BLY: This is exciting. Look at all these famous people stepping into the elevator to get to the *(your school's name)* Hall of Fame. My editors will love this story. *(Enter Chuck Yeager and Milton Hershey.)* There's Chuck Yeager. Chuck, how do you feel today?

CHUCK YEAGER: It's quite an honor to be inducted into the Hall of Fame. I haven't been this happy since I flew at Mach 1.

BLY: That's the speed of sound. As I recall, you were the first to break the sound barrier. And to think, people thought it was such a big deal that I was able to go around the world in fewer than 80 days. *(She turns to Milton Hershey.)* Sir, I don't believe we've ever met. I'm Nellie Bly, ace reporter.

MILTON HERSHEY: I'm Milton Hershey, chocolate king. Ever hear of the Hershey Bar and Chocolate Kisses? I created them. *(Yeager and Hershey step onto the elevator, and Nellie moves toward two women talking.)*

BLY: Here's Princess Ka'iulani, the last princess of Hawaii, and anthropologist Margaret Mead.

MARGARET MEAD: I've been talking to Princess Ka'iulani about her Hawaiian civilization. It is an interesting and exciting one. I would love to study it someday.

From *The Persona Book.* © 1997. Katherine Lallier and Nancy Marino. TIP. (800) 237-6124.

PRINCESS KA'IULANI:	But I'm sad to say that part of it is ending with me. I am the last Hawaiian princess.
BLY:	Margaret Mead, I'm glad that you were able to take time away from your study of primitive cultures to be here, and Princess Ka'iulani, it was good of you to come also.
PRINCESS KA'IULANI:	It's not every day we are inducted into the *(your school)* Hall of Fame. *(The women step toward the elevator.)*
GEORGE EASTMAN:	Wait. Before you all get into the elevator, I'd like to take your picture. I just invented this camera. *(They pose and he takes their picture.)*
BLY:	You must be George Eastman, founder of the Eastman Kodak Company. Can I have this picture for my newspaper?
EASTMAN:	Of course. Are we ready to go, or are we waiting for more people?
BLY:	We have to pick up some people on the second floor and some on the third.

(They all get into the elevator.)

EASTMAN:	Here's the second floor.

(Bly gets out to see if some people are coming in. She sees Tecumseh, Picotte, and Thoreau.)

BLY:	Here's Tecumseh, the great Shawnee leader.
TECUMSEH:	My name is actually Tecumtha. It means great panther crouching. The white people changed my name from Tecumtha to Tecumseh.
BLY:	And this is Susan LaFlesche Picotte, the first Native American women to graduate from medical school. What is your tribe?
SUSAN LaFLESCHE PICOTTE:	I am from the Omaha tribe.
TECUMSEH:	Medicine is a good thing to learn. In our tribe medicine men are valued. It is good for a woman to learn.

BLY: And here is Henry David Thoreau, the famous philosopher and writer.

HENRY DAVID THOREAU: I even left my home at beautiful Walden Pond to be inducted into the Hall of Fame.

BLY: Wait a minute. I see Captain Robert Smalls, the Civil War hero. He took a Confederate steamer filled with escaped slaves and ammunition and sailed it straight past the Confederate troops at Fort Sumter.

ROBERT SMALLS: That began my naval career. Before that I was a slave.

BLY: Congratulations on being picked for the *(your school)* Hall of Fame.

(They all get in.)

EASTMAN: Fourth floor is coming up.

(An old woman gets in. She is being escorted by a man.)

BLY: This is Grandma Moses. She began her painting career at age 70. Her American folk art really took off when she was in her 80s. How old are you now, Grandma?

GRANDMA MOSES: I'm 99. I just came in from a meeting with President Truman. You know, he grew up on a farm too.

BLY: Did you talk about politics?

GRANDMA: "No, ploughin'."

EASTMAN: We're going to the top floor now. We're heading straight to the *(your school)* Hall of Fame.

BLY: Did you have any problem getting here, Grandma Moses?

GRANDMA: No, this nice gentleman helped me. *(She turns to the young man who helped her.)* I didn't get your name, young man.

BENEDICT ARNOLD: My name is Benedict Arnold.

HERSHEY: Benedict Arnold, the infamous Revolutionary War traitor?

From *The Persona Book.* © 1997. Katherine Lallier and Nancy Marino. TIP. (800) 237-6124.

YEAGER: Hey, you can't be inducted into the Hall of Fame. I fought for my country, but you were a traitor to it.

(A loud jerk. The characters sway.)

PRINCESS KA'IULANI: What happened?

EASTMAN: We're stuck. The elevator isn't moving.

GRANDMA: Oh my goodness.

PICOTTE: Someone will help us. They will get us out.

BLY: What a great story: all these Hall of Famers stuck in an elevator.

SMALLS: We're all Hall of Famers except for Benedict Arnold. He can't possibly be in the Hall of Fame. He betrayed the United States of America and gave information to the British.

TECUMSEH: I fought on the side of the British. These white settlers came and took the land of my people. I think that this Benedict Arnold may be a hero after all—if, in fact, he tried to prevent these settlers from taking my land.

YEAGER: But he betrayed his own people. He was a general in the Revolutionary War, and he gave information to people on the other side.

TECUMSEH: Then you are right. He is no hero. A man who betrays his own people is no hero in my eyes.

ARNOLD: I wanted to be a hero. The life I led was not the life I had imagined.

THOREAU: "If one advances confidently in the direction of his dreams and lives the life he had imagined, he will meet with success unexpected in common hours."

ARNOLD: And if one doesn't lead the life he had imagined, it could lead to failure.

MEAD: This is all quite interesting. I could write a study on this some day. Although I usually study primitive cultures, it would be interesting to study how people stuck on an elevator act and behave.

(Thoreau starts to gasp for breath.)

PICOTTE: Move over, please. Let me near him. I'm a doctor.

THOREAU: I feel locked in. These man-made things—I miss being out near nature. I think of paddling my boat on Walden Pond surrounded by pines and oak woods.

PICOTTE: You'll be okay. Just take deep breaths.

PRINCESS KA'IULANI: I'm not feeling too well either. Can you help me?

PICOTTE: (*Examines her*) I don't think so. There's nothing that medicine can do for a broken heart. You need to go back to Hawaii and be its queen.

PRINCESS KA'IULANI: If only I could.

HERSHEY: Anyone hungry? I have lots of chocolate bars. (*He gives out chocolate bars.*)

EASTMAN: I'm good at fixing things. If I can get to the engine, maybe I can fix it.

SMALLS: I've been in worse situations on the high seas. I bet I could lift you through the top, and we could hold you there until you fix the motor.

YEAGER: I could give you a hand.

BLY: Me too.

(*Eastman fixes the elevator and it starts up. They ride to the last floor.*)

HERSHEY: Last stop for the Hall of Fame.

ARNOLD: I want to be in the Hall of Fame.

GRANDMA: I don't think you can.

TECUMSEH: It's only for heroes, for those who fought bravely.

MEAD: For those who helped their people.

BLY: I guess we are all American heroes.

(*They all walk away except for Benedict Arnold.*)

ARNOLD: All I ever really wanted out of life was to be a hero.

From *The Persona Book*. © 1997. Katherine Lallier and Nancy Marino. TIP. (800) 237-6124.

B. Activities and Games

The following activities incorporate role playing or provide a way of introducing students to the genre as well as the American heroes.

Dinner Guests

Here is a persona twist on the famous question, "Name five people you would want to invite for dinner." The students have to choose five people their persona would want for dinner, and, of course, they have to explain why. Encourage them to mix time periods, and choose people in many different professions. The concentration is not only on their own personas but on their classmates' personas. For them to be able to come up with their list of "dinner guests," they must be familiar with their classmates' and their own persona's likes, dislikes, personality traits, and professional accomplishments.

Scavenger Hunt

The scavenger hunt work sheet (see page 180), can be used to introduce students to their personas. By completing the scavenger hunt, students become familiar with a variety of heroes. This gives them background knowledge that allows them to make a more informed decision concerning who they wish to be for the persona projects. The work sheet is general enough to use with your personal biography selections.

Look Who's Talking: Bartlett's and Biographies

One of the best ways to identify with a famous person is to read his or her actual words and thoughts. It is a way to step into their shoes or creep under their skin. None of the subjects in this unit wrote an autobiography, but many wrote speeches, essays, and other expressions of their ideas.

Learning about historical personas is an excellent way to also learn about a popular reference tool: Bartlett's *Familiar Quotations*. Studying personas gives meaning to learning about this resource.

There are several ways to approach this endeavor. Ask students to look up their persona to see if there is a famous quotation and, if there is, to choose one that is meaningful to them. Because some of the personas do not appear in Bartlett's, another activity might be to match the personas with the quotes listed on the following handout (see page 181). This gives students a chance to hypothesize about who said what and to look up the correct answer through the book's author table of contents or the quotation index. After this exercise, students should be proficient in using Bartlett's and know a little bit more about some rather eloquent Americans. Bartlett's in also available on the Internet at http://www.columbia.edu/acis/bartleby/bartlett/ for those students who want to go online.

Name _____

BIOGRAPHY SCAVENGER HUNT

This is an opportunity to get to meet many great American men and women who changed the course of American history. This scavenger hunt will help you get to know the different people you will be studying.

1. Name as many biographies of Native Americans as you can find.

2. Which biographies are about U.S. presidents?

3. Name one person you know nothing about.

4. How many explorers can you discover?

5. Name one hero you think is a hard worker.

6. March about, and find some soldiers. Name at least two.

7. How many "Johns" can you name?

8. There are a few biographies about people who are living. Find one.

9. Many Americans have overcome their physical disabilities and limitations to achieve and to lead. Name a few and their accomplishments.

10. Name two Americans you believe were leaders.

11. Do not strike out on this one. Find at least one sports figure.

12. Habla Español? Name one person who could speak Spanish.

13. Name one person who you think has courage.

14. You named some presidents. Can you find some First Ladies?

15. Can you find at least five great African Americans?

16. As you fly through these biographies, can you spot a pilot?

17. Determination means you stick to a job until it is done. Who do you think may have been determined?

18. Find one American who goes by three names.

19. Who do you think was a kind person?

20. Which biography do you think will be the most interesting to you?

From *The Persona Book*. © 1997. Katherine Lallier and Nancy Marino. TIP. (800) 237-6124.

Student's Name _____

BARTLETT'S AND BIOGRAPHIES

Can you identify who said or wrote these famous quotations? Use a recent Bartlett's *Familiar Quotations* to verify your answers.

AMERICAN HEROES FOR OUR TIMES:

Louisa May Alcott   Amelia Earhart   Tecumseh
Mary McLeod Bethune   Theodore Roosevelt
Chief Joseph   Abraham Lincoln   Cesar Chavez
Elizabeth Cady Stanton   Henry David Thoreau

1. "From where the sun now stands, I will fight no more forever."

2. "Viva la huelga." (Long live the strike.)

3. "Sell a country! Why not sell the air, the clouds and the great sea, as well as the earth? Did not the Great Spirit make them all for the use of his children?"

4. "What does the Negro want? His answer is very simple. He wants only what all other Americans want. He wants opportunity to make real what the Declaration of Independence and the Constitution and the Bill of Rights say, what the Four Freedoms establish. While he knows these ideals are open to no man completely, he wants only his equal chance to obtain them."

5. "As I would not be a *slave*, so I would not be a *master*. This expresses my idea of democracy."

6. "We hold these truths to be self-evident, that all men are created equal."

7. "Dreams are the touchstones of our characters."

8. "To waste, to destroy, our natural resources, to skin and exhaust the land instead of using it so as to increase its usefulness, will result in undermining in the days of our children the very prosperity which we ought by right to hand down to them amplified and developed."

9. "Christmas won't be Christmas without any presents."

10. "Courage is the price that life exacts for granting peace. The soul that knows it not, knows no release from little things; knows not the livid loneliness of fear, nor mountain heights where bitter joy can hear the sound of wings."

"Look Who's Talking" handout answer key:

1. Chief Joseph	6. Elizabeth Cady Stanton
2. Cesar Chavez	7. Henry David Thoreau
3. Tecumseh	8. Theodore Roosevelt
4. Mary McLeod Bethune	9. Louisa May Alcott
5. Abraham Lincoln	10. Amelia Earhart

Star Search

To motivate your students or to have the children motivate one another or another class, play "Star Search."

After students have read their biography, have them name eight to 10 important facts, events, or highlights about their persona's life. Using poster paper, list the facts without revealing the persona's identity. At the bottom of the poster, attach an envelope for students to put their guesses in. Decorate the poster with gold stars and American flags.

This activity promotes the fine art of skimming. It encourages students to look closely at the table of contents, the index, the cover, and the captions under photographs.

"Star Search" gives focus to a biography readathon. Students have direction as they read through numerous biographies. "Star Search" can also be used as a culminating activity for students to create for one another and to use at the "Living Museum."

The following "star searches" can be used as models for your students to follow or by the teacher as an introductory activity.

STAR SEARCH #1

1. I was born in 1820 or 1821.
2. I was the sixth of 11 children.
3. I was owned by Edward Brodas.
4. Two of my sisters were sold to other plantations.
5. In 1835, I was almost killed when the master threw a metal weight at a runaway slave.
6. With two of my brothers, I escaped to Pennsylvania.
7. I helped lead 300 slaves to freedom via the Underground Railroad.
8. Some people began to call me Moses.
9. I was wanted "dead or alive."
10. I was past 90 when I died on March 10, 1913.

Who am I? (Harriet Tubman)

STAR SEARCH #2

1. I was born November 18, 1945, in Oklahoma.
2. I have six brothers and four sisters.
3. I worked hard for equal rights for my people.
4. My tribe was the largest of the five civilized tribes.
5. My people walked what is now known as the Trail of Tears.
6. In 1979, I was in a terrible car accident.
7. I govern more than 120,000 people.
8. My last name may sound strange, but in my tribe 200 years ago it was given to those with a high military rank.
9. I am always battling poverty, discrimination, and discouragement.
10. In 1986, I was American Indian Woman of the Year. In 1987, I became Woman of the Year.

Who am I? (Wilma Mankiller)

STAR SEARCH #3

1. I was born in 1854 to a family with little money.
2. I started working at age 13.
3. I searched for a hobby and discovered I was interested in photography.
4. I loved my hobby, but it was expensive and required a lot of heavy equipment.
5. I tried to invent easier ways to take pictures.
6. I invented film.
7. I invented the Brownie—and I don't mean a piece of chocolate or a young Girl Scout. I made it for kids.
8. When I became a millionaire, I helped the community by starting a dental clinic, a hospital, and the Rochester Symphony.
9. I loved camping and took home movies on an African safari.
10. I died in 1932.

Who am I? (George Eastman)

Walk in My Shoes

After students are familiar with their biographies, they will identify the obstacles and accomplishments in their persona's lives. They may create a simple game that will help others learn about their chosen personas. Samples are offered, but this activity can be done for any persona.

Students need to cut out footprints, or "shoe prints," to place on the floor.

The student must then list important setbacks and accomplishments of their persona. Each accomplishment should be placed on a separate index card. A game direction such as "Move ahead one place" or "Move ahead two places" should be included on the bottom of the card. The same should be done for obstacles, but the game direction should move the player back a space.

This activity is noncompetitive and a different way to introduce others to the different personas that are being studied. Use this game as a demonstration area or exhibit in the "Living Museum."

Below is a sample of accomplishments and setbacks in one personas' life.

Benjamin Banneker

Although Benjamin was born free in 1731, he had little choice but to tend tobacco to support himself. This was an obstacle in his early years.

Move back one space.

Benjamin was naturally curious about astronomy. He taught himself all about the subject, and his determination led him to publish the first almanac by an African American man. These attributes helped him throughout his life.

Move ahead two spaces.

Benjamin could not find a publisher who would print his almanac, because they did not trust his ability. This was a terrible obstacle.

Move back two spaces.

Benjamin was finally able to get his almanac published, but he was not satisfied. He realized many African Americans were enslaved and even more were unable to read. Benjamin had the courage to write to Thomas Jefferson and tell him that slavery must be abolished.

Move ahead one space.

Benjamin was hired to help survey the nation's new capital, which would later be named Washington, D.C. This was a great accomplishment for any man—black or white—in the eighteenth century.

Move ahead one space.

Congratulations! You've walked in Benjamin Banneker's shoes!

Giant Time Line

Create a giant time line so that students can examine their personas' relationships to one another and historical events. Include the dates of birth and death of all the personas as well as important dates in history. Use a computer-software program, such as *Timeliner*, by Tom Snyder. Simply enter the dates, and let the software create the time line. Display it around your library or classroom.

Media Blitz: Read All About It!

If you visit your local newsstand, you will notice many magazines dedicated to interesting personalities. From *Us* to *People*, there is a great interest in celebrities. Create your own tabloid magazine starring the personas of your class. Choose a cover personality or, better yet, a romantic couple, such as Charles and Anne Morrow Lindbergh. Do not forget to include cover highlights, such as chocolate recipes by Milton Hershey and news of Matt Henson's latest expedition. Use E. B. White as your publisher or copy editor, and include feature articles on Sam Houston's latest adventure and Alvin Ailey's newest choreography. Include lots of photographs and illustrations, and let George Eastman be your photo editor. Use a desktop publisher such as Microsoft's *Creative Writer* for a professional-looking finished product. Your class magazine is sure to be more interesting than anything on the newsstands today.

The Funnies

Display several of Quackenbush's biographies, such as *Don't You Dare Shoot That Bear: A Story of Theodore Roosevelt* or *Mark Twain? What Kind of Name Is That? A Story of Samuel Langhorne Clemens*. Quackenbush punctuates his biographies with a series of amusing cartoons on the subject's life. Offer your illustrators the opportunity to create a comic strip based on their persona's life.

Public Television Presents . . . "Biographies"

One of the most popular series on PBS is "Biography." It explores the lives of fascinating people past and present. Give your students the chance to create their own episode for this television series. Children who have access to a camcorder would need to create a storyboard and develop a script for their five- to 10-minute production.

Database of Heroes

Use a database program to create a listing of students' personas. An easy-to-use database program is Claris Corp.'s *ClarisWorks*. Set up the fields, and let the students type in the information for their own personas. Some suggestions for fields in the database are: Name, Birth Year, Year of Death, Occupation, Attributes, and Obstacles. By searching the database students can make comparisons. For example, they may perform a search to discover how many people were born in a certain year or how many people had the term *courageous* as one of their attributes.

A commercially available database is MECC's *History Makers*. It includes profiles of more than 200 outstanding Americans from various ethnic groups. Students can play a who's-who game or search the database.

C. Displays

Trading Cards

The popularity of trading cards in this country is undeniable. At first the cards were limited to sports heroes—specifically baseball players. Trading cards now cover a range of hobbies and interests from endangered species to *Star Trek*. Biography trading cards also exist and are usually attached to a theme such as great African Americans, inventors, or famous women. Our twist is to have students make biography trading cards and to make them as large as 12 by 18 inches.

The front of the card should include the name of the person as well as a portrait or action scene. The back of the card should include the following information:

Name

Persona's dates

Place of birth

Occupation

Obstacles in life

Attributes

Title of biography

Author of biography

Summary of the person's life

Display the trading cards in your classroom or library to create a Hero Hall of Fame. When the display is over, the cards make a wonderful gift to the school library. Students from other classes can—and probably will—browse through them to make their own biography selections.

Great American Quilt

Have students create a patch for their persona. The patch could be of cloth, but it could also simply be a small, square 8-by-8-inch piece of construction paper. Illustrations should include things important to each student's persona. For example, Susan LaFlesche Picotte's patch could include symbols from her Native American tribe as well as a medical symbol.

How to Make a Hero Sandwich

Throughout this unit, the focus is not just on these select Americans but on people with worthwhile attributes who should be emulated. So often one hears that today's children have no role models, no genuine heroes. Our history is filled with people who had integrity, faith, perseverance, and altruistic visions. These people need to be rediscovered, and their attributes identified and analyzed. It must also be noted that these attributes were forged in the face of obstacles. The qualities of heroes can only be measured based on the challenges they faced head-on.

Begin your lesson by defining the word *attribute*. Share with students the famous story of George Washington and the cherry tree. Aliki wrote a short picture book entitled *George and the Cherry Tree* that can be used for this example. Elicit from the students what attributes young George exhibited.

Brainstorm with your students to come up with a list of positive attributes. Qualities may include . . .

honesty	loyalty
determination	fairness
courage	leadership
intelligence	thoughtfulness
common sense	tolerance
kindness	perseverance
industriousness	consideration
generosity	faith
patience	integrity

Read Golenbock's picture book *Teammates*. It is the true and touching story of Pee Wee Reese and Jackie Robinson during the 1947 baseball season. Robinson was the first African American man to play on a major-league team, and he suffered much abuse from fans, opposing players, and his own teammates. Southern-born Reese publicly declared his support of Robinson. Together these men helped change the game of baseball for the better. The qualities exhibited in this book will reinforce the idea of attributes for your children and give them two more American heroes to emulate.

Using the list as a guide, allow students to work in a group to create their own idea of a perfect "hero sandwich."

An irresistible sandwich may sound something like this. . . .

> Between two slices of intelligence and hard work, add a generous portion of determination and perseverance, a helping of honesty, a generous portion of generosity with a dash of courage and fairness. Do not forget a few dabs of kindness and a side order of patience.

Children can illustrate their "heroes" for a bulletin-board display.

Book Jackets

Unless you are fortunate enough to receive funding for new books, it is more than likely you will be using some worn biographies. If only older titles are available to you, fear not. As long as you have checked the accuracy of the information and avoid stereotypical depictions, you probably have several gems in your collection. Many classic Jean Fritz titles are more than 20 years old but still excellent.

Your problem may lie in getting children excited about old books. This is your opportunity to give that age-old lesson about not judging a book by its cover—or lack of one. Give your students the opportunity to design dust jackets for these well-worn books.

After students have read their biographies, have them design a cover illustration. They will also need to include the title, the author's name, and the name of the illustrator in their design. Students will also learn about what information needs to appear on a book's spine: title, author, publisher, and call number. Give students the task of writing a book blurb or summary for the inside cover, and ask them to write a brief "biography" of the dust-jacket illustrator—themselves—on the back inside cover. The covers will look professional if you laminate them or use plastic book-jacket protectors. The biography collection will be rejuvenated with this activity.

Wagon Wheels

Biography wagon wheels help students understand the relationship between a person and the society in which that person lives. The student learns that a person acts or reacts to the historical and societal events that occurred in that person's life. The students also come to understand the historical time period.

Have students trace a large wagon wheel and draw a picture of their persona in the center. After each student decides on the most important events that happened in his or her persona's life, the student should write them in the spaces between the spikes. The spikes are characteristics of that person. The rim is events that took place in society or the themes that influenced that person. For example, for Louisa May Alcott, the spaces between the spikes might include her falling into the duck pond, her trip to Europe, her being a nurse during the Civil War, her first publication. The spikes may contain qualities such as determination and intelligence. The rim would be filled with events such as the Civil War and the women's suffrage movement and with themes such as the oppression of women.

D. Spectacles

The Living Museum

Many of the activities that have already been presented can be part of your Living Museum. "Walk in My Shoes," "How to Make a Hero Sandwich," "Star Search," and the "Great American Quilt" can all appear at the exhibition.

If you choose to create a Living Museum, nothing is more impressive than everyone dressing as their personas. As a spectator, it is quite thrilling to come face-to-face with frontiersman Sam Houston or Cherokee leader Wilma Mankiller. To see aviator Amelia Earhart speaking with General Colin Powell is exciting for audience and performer alike. It is also the final step in the student's truly becoming the chosen persona.

An interesting display at your Living Museum is the "artifacts collection." A group of personas should select two or three items that represent their chosen hero. For instance, Princess Ka'iulani might be symbolized by a lei for her native Hawaii, a crown for her royal station, and a book of Robert Louis Stevenson poems for its significance in her life. Animal-rights activist Henry Bergh may be represented by a nesting doll to show his diplomatic connection to Russia and a flier or poster about animal abuse from the ASPCA. Finally, President Theodore Roosevelt can be symbolized with his namesake, the teddy bear, a big stick (remember the famous quote about walking softly and carrying a big stick?), and a poster of a national park (Mount Rushmore is a good choice).

Use another group of personas as living statues. Design a giant button for spectators to press. When the button is "activated," have students behave as robotic versions of their personas. They can tell an important accomplishment or say a famous quote before they return to their frozen state. Franklin Delano Roosevelt can come to life and say, "December 7, 1941: a day that will live in infamy." He can offer a quick synopsis as to why before he freezes. Chief Joseph can explain the plight of Native Americans before he says his famous quote, "I will fight no more forever."

Select a day when other classes and parents can visit your Living Museum. They are sure to learn a lot about the people who have made the United States a great nation.

Bibliography

Adler, David. *Martin Luther King, Jr.: Free at Last*. New York: Holiday House, 1986.

———. *A Picture Book of Harriet Tubman*. New York: Holiday House, 1992.

Altman, Susan. *Extraordinary Black Americans from Colonial to Contemporary Times*. Chicago: Childrens Press, 1989.

Avery, Susan, and Linda Skinner. *Extraordinary American Indians*. Chicago: Childrens Press, 1992.

Ayres, Carter. *Chuck Yeager: Fighter Pilot*. Minneapolis, Minn.: Lerner, 1988.

Banta, Melissa. *Colin Powell*. Junior World Biographies. New York: Chelsea Juniors, 1995.

Bartlett, John. *Familiar Quotations*. ed. by Emily Morison Beck. Boston: Little, Brown, 1980.

Burleigh, Robert. *Flight: The Journey of Charles Lindbergh*. New York: Philomel, 1991.

Burnford, Betty. *Chocolate by Hershey: A Story About Milton Hershey*. Minneapolis, Minn.: Carolrhoda Books, 1994.

Carpenter, Angelica Shirley, and Jean Shirley. *Frances Hodgson Burnett: Beyond the Secret Garden*. Minneapolis, Minn.: Lerner, 1990.

Carruth, Ella Kaiser. *She Wanted to Read: The Story of Mary McLeod Bethune*. Nashville, Tenn.: Abingdon Press, 1981.

Chadwick, Roxane. *Amelia Earhart*. The Achievers Series. Minneapolis, Minn.: Lerner, 1987.

Colman, Penny. *Mother Jones and the March of the Mill Children*. Brookfield, Conn.: Millbrook, 1994.

Collins, David. *To the Point: A Story About E. B. White*. Minneapolis, Minn.: Carolrhoda Books, 1989.

Connell, Kate. *These Lands Are Ours: Tecumseh's Fight for the Old Northwest*. Austin, Tex.: Raintree, 1993.

Dell, Pamela. *I. M. Pei: Designer of Dreams*. Chicago: Childrens Press, 1993.

Emerson, Kathy Lynn. *Making Headlines: A Biography of Nellie Bly*. A People in Focus Book. Minneapolis, Minn.: Dillon, 1989.

Ferris, Jeri. *Arctic Explorer: The Story of Matthew Henson*. Minneapolis, Minn.: Carolrhoda Books, 1989.

———. *Go Free or Die: A Story About Harriet Tubman*. Minneapolis, Minn.: Carolrhoda Books, 1988.

———. *Native American Doctor: The Story of Susan LaFlesche Picotte*. Minneapolis, Minn.: Carolrhoda Books, 1991.

———. *What Are You Figuring Now?: A Story About Benjamin Banneker*. Minneapolis, Minn.: Carolrhoda Books, 1988.

Freedman, Russell. *Lincoln: A Photobiography*. New York: Clarion Books, 1987.

Fritz, Jean. *Bully for You, Teddy Roosevelt!* New York: Putnam, 1990.

———. *The Double Life of Pocahontas.* New York: Putnam, 1983.

———. *Make Way for Sam Houston.* New York: Putnam, 1986.

———. *Traitor: The Case of Benedict Arnold.* New York: Putnam, 1981.

———. *What's the Big Idea, Ben Franklin?* New York: Coward, McCann & Geoghegan, 1976.

———. *You Want Women to Vote, Lizzie Stanton?* New York: Putnam, 1995.

Giblin, James Cross. *Edith Wilson: The Woman Who Ran the White House.* New York: Viking, 1992.

———. *George Washington: A Picture Book Biography.* New York: Scholastic, 1992.

———. *Thomas Jefferson: A Picture Book Biography.* New York: Scholastic, 1994.

Giff, Patricia Reilly. *Laura Ingalls Wilder: Growing Up in the Little House.* New York: Viking Kestrel, 1987.

Gilman, Michael. *Matthew Henson.* Black Americans of Achievement. New York: Chelsea House, 1988.

Glassman, Bruce. *Wilma Mankiller: Chief of the Cherokee Nation.* The Library of Famous Women. New York: Blackbirch Press, 1992.

Golenbock, Peter. *Teammates.* San Diego, Calif.: Harcourt Brace Jovanovich, 1990.

Haskins, Jim. *I Have a Dream: The Life and Words of Martin Luther King, Jr.* Brookfield, Conn.: Millbrook, 1992.

Kent, Zachary. *Tecumseh.* Cornerstones of Freedom. Chicago: Childrens Press, 1992.

Landau, Elaine. *Colin Powell: Four-Star General.* New York: Franklin Watts, 1991.

Loeper, John. *Crusade for Kindness: Henry Bergh and the ASPCA.* New York: Atheneum, 1991.

Malone, Mary. *Milton Hershey: Chocolate King.* Champaign, Ill.: Garrard, 1971.

McKissack, Patricia. *Mary McLeod Bethune: A Great American Educator.* Chicago: Childrens Press, 1985.

Meltzer, Milton. *Mary McLeod Bethune: Voice of Black Hope.* New York: Viking Kestrel, 1987.

Mitchell, Barbara. *Click: A Story About George Eastman.* Minneapolis, Minn.: Carolrhoda Books, 1986.

Moutoussamy-Ashe, Jeanne. *Daddy and Me: A Photo Story of Arthur Ashe and His Daughter Camera.* New York: Alfred A. Knopf, 1993.

O'Neal, Zibby. *Grandma Moses: Painter of Rural America.* New York: Viking Kestrel, 1986.

Pinkney, Andrea Davis. *Alvin Ailey.* New York: Hyperion Books for Children, 1993.

———. *Dear Benjamin Banneker.* San Diego, Calif.: Gulliver Books, 1994.

Provensen, Alice. *The Buck Stops Here.* New York: HarperCollins, 1990.

———. *My Fellow Americans.* New York: Browndeer Press, 1995.

Quackenbush, Robert. *Don't You Dare Shoot That Bear! A Story of Theodore Roosevelt.* New York: Simon & Schuster, 1982.

———. *Mark Twain? What Kind of Name Is That? A Story of Samuel Langhorne Clemens.* New Jersey: Prentice-Hall, 1984.

Reef, Catherine. *Benjamin Davis, Jr. African American Soldiers.* Frederick, Md.: Twenty First Century Books, 1992.

———. *Henry David Thoreau: A Neighbor to Nature. Earth's Keepers.* Frederick, Md.: Twenty First Century Books, 1992.

Roberts, Naurice. *Cesar Chavez and La Causa.* Chicago: Childrens Press, 1986.

St. George, Judith. *Crazy Horse.* New York: G. P. Putnam's Sons, 1994.

Sanford, William. *Chief Joseph: Nez Percé Warrior. Native American Leaders of the Wild West.* Hillside, N.J.: Enslow, 1994.

Sauders, Susan. *Margaret Mead: The World Was Her Family.* New York: Viking Kestrel, 1987.

Shumate, Jane. *Soujourner Truth and the Voice of Freedom.* Brookfield, Conn.: Millbrook, 1991.

Sinnott, Susan. *Extraordinary Asian Pacific Americans.* Chicago: Childrens Press, 1993.

———. *Extraordinary Hispanic Americans.* Chicago: Childrens Press, 1991.

Stanley, Fay. *The Last Princess: The Story of Princess Ka'iulani of Hawaii.* New York: Aladdin Books, 1991.

Towle, Wendy. *The Real McCoy: The Life of an African-American Inventor.* New York: Scholastic, 1993.

Weissberg, Ted. *Arthur Ashe. Black Americans of Achievement.* New York: Chelsea House, 1991.

Winter, Jeanette. *Diego.* New York: Alfred A. Knopf, 1991.

Software

ClarisWorks. IBM. Claris Corp., Santa Clara, Calif.

Creative Writer. IBM. Microsoft, Redmond, Wash.

History Makers. IBM. MECC, Minneapolis, Minn.

Timeliner. IBM. Tom Snyder Productions, Watertown, Mass.

About the Authors

Katherine Grimes Lallier, is a library media specialist at the Robert W. Carbonaro Elementary School in Valley Stream, New York, where the projects in this book have been implemented. She received her Master of Library Science from St. John's University, Queens, New York. Kate resides on Long Island with her husband, John, and her two children, James and Erin.

Nancy Robinson Marino, is an assistant professor on the library faculty at C. W. Post Campus of Long Island University in New York. She has a Master of Library Science from St. John's University, Queens, New York, and will receive a Masters of Science in Computers in Education from Long Island University in May 1997. She lives in Amityville, Long Island, with her husband, Sal.

From Teacher Ideas Press

Heard About These Books?

COOPERATIVE LEARNING ACTIVITIES IN THE LIBRARY MEDIA CENTER
Lesley S. J. Farmer

Equip yourself with strategies to implement cooperative learning activities that will help students assimilate information skills and content knowledge while sharpening critical-thinking skills. **Grades 6–12**.
xiv, 184p. ISBN 0-87287-799-X

TECHNOLOGY ACROSS THE CURRICULUM: Activities and Ideas
Marilyn J. Bazeli and James L. Heintz

Link literature to technology with these 75 classroom-tested, ready-to-use activities. Simple instructions and reproducible activity sheets for video, audio, and multimedia production; computer projects; and photographic/transparency activities are included. **Grades 1–12**.
x, 207p. 8½x11 paper ISBN 1-56308-444-9

THE REFERENCE INFORMATION SKILLS GAME
Myram Forney Tunnicliff and Susan Sheldon Soenen

Students go beyond mere fact-finding to designing and recording search strategies with *The Reference Information Skills Game*. With search maps, award badges, and search strategy suggestions—activities help students acquire and sharpen reference, information retrieval, and problem-solving skills on a daily basis. **Grades 4–9**.
xvi, 107p. 8½x11 paper ISBN 1-56308-296-9

CREATING SUCCESS IN THE CLASSROOM: Visual Organizers and How to Use Them
Patti Tarquin and Sharon Walker

Visual frameworks—or graphic organizers—offer you a fresh approach to classroom activities and are designed to be implemented at a moment's notice, with little or no preparation. The authors describe such techniques as flow charts, story maps, Venn diagrams, frameworks for webbing, KWL charts, and semantic feature analysis. **All levels**.
xiii, 235p. 8½x11 paper ISBN 1-56308-437-6

THE MINI-SOCIETY WORKBOOK: Everything You Need to Create a Mini-Society in Your Classroom
Kathleen D. Fletcher

As members of their own classroom mini-society, students learn valuable life skills and develop interdisciplinary abilities while gaining information about economics, government issues, world societies and cultures, careers, consumer issues, real-world math, language arts, creative expression, and fine arts. **Grades 3–9**.
xi, 149p. 8½x11 paper ISBN 1-56308-347-7

READERS THEATRE FOR CHILDREN: Scripts and Script Development
Mildred Knight Laughlin and Kathy Howard Latrobe

Looking for a new way to introduce your students to good books? These reproducible scripts of classics that appeal to children and suggested scenes from contemporary books that students can use to write their own scripts will spark interest while improving reading, speaking, and writing skills. Accompanying activities show how readers theater works. **Grades 4–6**.
xi, 131p. 8½x11 paper ISBN 0-87287-753-1

For a FREE catalog or to order these or any Teacher Ideas Press titles, please contact:
Teacher Ideas Press
Dept. B28 • P.O. Box 6633 • Englewood, CO 80155-6633
Phone: 1-800-237-6124, ext. 1 • Fax: 303-220-8843 • E-mail: lu-books@lu.com